The story of the 593rd Engineer Boat & Shore Regiment

OPERATION BORNEO

The last, untold story of the War in the Pacific, 1945

GERARD R. CASE and JAMES A. POUNDS

First published by Author House 06/10/04

ISBN: 1-4184-1830-7 (e-book)
ISBN: 1-4184-1831-5 (Paperback)

This book is printed on acid free paper.

Credits:

Design and Production: Gerard R. Case
Typesetting and editorial: April Mostek

**Books by
GERARD R. CASE**

Fossil Shark and Fish remains of North America
Fossils Illustrated
Handbook of Fossil Collecting
Fossil Sharks, a pictorial review
A Pictorial Guide to Fossils

This book is in memory of all the American fighting men and women in the Army, the Navy, the Marines and the Air Force, who lost their lives defending freedom in World War II—1941-1945.

ボルネオ作戦

The following veterans of the 593rd EBSR
who fought on Borneo have passed away since
this book was started in 1998. It is a darn
shame that they are not around to see their
story in World War II being told:

Loren W. Aicher of Company A, 2003
Grover S. Black of Company A, 2000
Dwaine Burke of Company A, 2003
Mario Caporiccio, 1999
James P. Igoe, Company A, 1999
Donald Reddin of Company B, 2000
Anthony DeBlasie of Company B, 2001
John Cunningham of Company B, 2004

Cover illustration: An American landing craft unloading Australian
Soldiers on the beach at Balikpapan, Borneo, July 1, 1945

ADDENDUM
(FOR CHAPTER 6, BRUNEI BAY)

Tech Sergeant Danny Caparella standing over an attacking Jap soldier that he killed during the "Banzai" charge on Labuan Island, June 21, 1945. By shooting through the canvas of his tent, Caparella saved the life of his sleeping tent mate, Tech Sgt. Tony DeBlasie, as well as himself.

DEDICATION

The authors of this book wish to dedicate this work to their brothers, who also served in the military, in wartime, for the United States of America.

S 1/c James Sanford Case, Jr.
U.S. Navy 1938-1946

Fought the Japanese from battleships in the Pacific as a Fire Controlman. When he left the Navy in 1946, he had attained the rank of Chief Petty Officer. (1916- 1989)

Cpl. Isham Frank Pounds, Jr.
U.S. Army 1943-1946

Fought with the 3rd Army under General Patton and worked half-tracks across the European Theater of Operations in the 14th Armored Division at Omaha Beach and the Battle of the Bulge.

FOREWORD

World War II was a long, costly and devastating event. Many stories have been written about the successes and failures of the campaigns in Africa, Europe, Asia and on the islands and waters of the oceans. The acts of valor of many outstanding individuals have been documented. The histories of the performance of many fighting units of all sizes in the various theaters of operations in the air, on and under the sea and on the land have been written.

There are many stories yet to be written about the contributions that were made by other American service men and women to the ultimate defeat of the Axis powers. This story is one then, a tale of the exploits of the 593rd Engineer Boat and Shore Regiment of the 3rd Engineer Special Brigade of the United States Army. It is a belated tribute to the 3,000 Amphibs of the 593rd who were an integral part of the combined Allied forces that engaged the Japanese in the Southwest Pacific Theater.

The story focuses on the men of Companies A, B and C of the 593rd who supported the 9th Australian Division on the Island of Borneo, the last major battlefield of World War II. The surrender of the enemy Japanese forces on Borneo stopped the spread of the "evil Empire of Japan" in their advance in the South West Pacific toward New Zealand and the Australian Continent.

The authors have woven a remarkable set of photographs, interviews and anecdotes into a fascinating story about the history and exploits of the Amphibs: The unique contribution of these fighting men to the ultimate defeat of the Japanese Empire is hereby recognized and is given its appropriate place in the history of the U.S. forces in World War II.

Rogers B. Finch, Brigadier General
Army of the United States, Retired
23 December 1998

INTRODUCTION

We have made our volume a study of the last three major amphibious assault landings of World War II because most readers have not heard of the Australians' sacrifices in recapturing the island of Borneo from the Japanese. The battles waged by the Australians, with the help of the Amphibious Engineers, the U.S. Navy and U.S. Air Corps, are seldom mentioned in volumes covering the military action in the Southwest Pacific Theater of Operations.

A recent publication "Tarakan, An Australian Tragedy" (1997) by Dr. Peter Stanley of the Australian War Memorial at Canberra, Australia, describes the battle for this island and the cost in Australian soldiers to recapture this piece of Dutch property. However, this book does not even mention the services of the 593rd Engineer Boat & Shore Regiment provided in this operation.

In the latest volume written of the war in the Southwest Pacific "MacArthur's Jungle War," (1998) by Stephen R. Taaffe, no mention is made of the 593rd Engineer Boat & Shore Regiment and the actions they participated with the Australians in Recapturing Borneo.

Our purpose here is to tell of the part the 593rd EB&SR played in the support of the 7th and 9th Australian divisions in the three major beachhead assaults in Borneo: Tarakan Island; Brunei Bay and Labuan Island and Balikpapan: We have noted the support given by the 307th Heavy Bomber Group that provided air support for the operations. In addition, we have given credit to one destroyer, the USS Charrette, that provided naval fire power for neutralizing gun positions and fortifications in close support of the assault landings.

The Third Engineer Special Brigade of which the 593rd Engineer Boat & Shore Regiment was a part, was activated at Camp Edwards, Massachusetts between the 6th and 12th of August 1942. As fate would have it, the war in the Pacific with Japan ended just three years later during this 6th to 12th of August 1945 period.

On the third anniversary of the formation of the Third Special Brigade, the brigade celebrated the completion of sixty beachhead landings on enemy-held shores. In the Bismarck Archipelago; Talasea and Gasmata; in New Guinea; Yalau, Aitape, Madang, Alexishafen, Wakde Island, Karkar Island, Noemfoor Island, Cape Opmari, Sansapor and Soepiori Island; In the Northern Philippines; Lingayen Gulf and Apparri; In the Southern Philippines; Zamboanga, Malabang-Parang, Mindanao River, The Davao Area, Luayou, Balut Island, San Augustin, Augusan River, and the Sulu Archipelago and in Borneo; Tarakan Island, Brunei Bay, Labuan Island and Balikpapan. There were also lesser landings within these major assault landings.

General MacArthur, Commander of the Allied Forces in the Southwest Pacific Theater of Operations, had promised the people of the Philippine Islands that he would return and every action in New Guinea and the Dutch East Indies was aimed at fulfilling this promise at the earliest possible date. His methods were to "leap frog" up the coast of New Guinea, bypassing Japanese strongholds isolating them and using Australian troops to "mop up." Borneo became one of the bypassed areas and one that was left for the Australians to neutralize, while MacArthur and the American troops moved into the Philippine Islands to make good his promise of "I Shall Return."

We are indebted to many members of the 593rd Engineer Boat & Shore Regiment of the 3rd Engineer Special Brigade for firsthand accounts of their personal experiences while fighting in Borneo. There are also stories of Australians and their accounts of the fighting to recapture Borneo from the Japanese.

Our special thanks go out to the servicemen who submitted pictures and other data for the chapter dedicated to the men who fought on the beaches and in the jungles. Without the help of these men, who were there, we would only have a story relating the facts of a military operation in a far off corner of the Southwest Pacific Ocean.

We wish to thank especially Sabah's Chief Minister, Datuk Harris bin Mohamed Salleh, for his contribution of pictures and details of modern Labuan Island and the State of Sabah (formerly British North Borneo).

In this volume, the usage of the nicknames Jap(s) and Nip(s) were commonly used by all the Allies during World War II, when the world was at war with the then Empire of Japan. Now that the present government of Japan is a democracy, these names are no longer applicable. Our usage of these nicknames are pertinent to our stories dealing with the war years in Borneo, particularly the first-hand accounts that we are including.

Many of the photos and the data from official orders were gleaned from the records in the National Archives in Washington, D.C. We are indeed very grateful for the help received from the Australians and from fellow American soldiers who were all veterans of the Borneo campaigns. Your help in making this story a tribute to those fighting men of both nations that fought, suffered and died for a cause in the steamy, insect-ridden, equatorial jungles of Borneo, to you, we extend our heartfelt thanks!

Operation Borneo was an Australian operation where thousands of Australian diggers and sappers died in their efforts to take this island back from the Japanese. It is well-known that the Australian soldiers gave their lives to liberate the people of Borneo, particularly at Tarakan Island. On this small island the Australians lost two hundred forty fighting men in the Oboe I engagement (Stanley 1997). (See pp. 109-110)

The Australians fought from one end of Borneo to the other in 1945. Many more of their men were killed liberating Brunei Bay, British North Borneo, Weston, Beaufort, Jesselton and Balikpapan. At Kuching they liberated several hundred British prisoners in a Japanese prison camp.

This is a tribute to those brave and valiant members of the Australian Army, Navy and Air Force, but it is also a recognition, long over due, of the allies of the Australians on Borneo, the Americans. Here we describe for the reader, historically, the part played by the American soldiers, sailors and airmen who fought and sometimes died alongside their Australian counterparts. This is the story of the combined efforts of the recapture of Borneo from the Japanese.

We recognize the sacrifices of the Australians, but here we wish to give rightful recognition to those three thousand or so Americans who also served and fought alongside their Australian brothers. They, the Americans, brought the Australian troops to Borneo, first to Tarakan, then to Labuan Island and Brunei Bay and finally to Balikpapan and landed them on the beaches in their LCMs, LSTs, LCIs and other troop landing craft. The LCMs of the Amphibious Engineers played a vital role in their ability to carry Australian troops to the enemy camps up the rivers.

We have given credit to other fighting units that played a crucial role in the recapture of Borneo; the 307th "Long Rangers," a heavy B24 Bomber Group who made many bomb runs over the targeted beaches in order to eliminate as many guns and fortifications as possible prior to the landings. Their bombing of enemy positions saved many lives. Our naval units were given recognition for their work in beach bombardment with their heavy guns and their naval aircraft. The USS Charrette was particularly active in the Brunei Bay and Balikpapan areas.

Our volume is about the role of the Amphibious Engineers in the defeat of the Japanese troops on Borneo. The men, of the 593rd Engineer Boat & Shore Regiment of the 3rd Engineer Special Brigade, including Headquarters, "A", "B", "C" Companies; Regimental Medical Detachments; The Signal Detachment; The Engineer Maintenance Units; and the Amphibious Tractor Units. Each of these units played a vital role in the three Borneo landings.

The Authors.

THE WHITE HOUSE
WASHINGTON

TO MEMBERS OF THE UNITED STATES ARMY EXPEDITIONARY
FORCES:

You are a soldier of the United States Army.

You have embarked for distant places where the war is being fought.

Upon the outcome depends the freedom of your lives: the freedom of the lives of those you love—your fellow-citizens—your people.

Never were the enemies of freedom more tyrannical, more arrogant, more brutal.

Yours is a God-fearing, proud, courageous people, which, throughout its history, has put its freedom under God before all other purposes.

We who stay at home have our duties to perform—duties owed in many parts to you. You will be supported by the whole force and power of this Nation. The victory you win will be a victory of all the people—common to them all.

You bear with you the hope, the confidence, the gratitude and the prayers of your family, your fellow-citizens, and your President—

Franklin D. Roosevelt

Contents

ADDENDUM iv

DEDICATION v

FOREWORD vi

INTRODUCTION vii

CHAPTER 1 1
History of the 593rd EB&SR:

CHAPTER 2 10
Those Who Served

CHAPTER 3 25
Australians on Borneo

CHAPTER 4 34
The Bombing Of Borneo

CHAPTER 5 39
The Tarakan Invasion

CHAPTER 6 57
Brunei Bay

CHAPTER 7 84
Balikpapan

CHAPTER 8 99
Japanese Surrender On Borneo

CHAPTER 9 106
In Memorium

CHAPTER 10..**117**
    Borneo Today

CHAPTER 11..**122**
    Japanese Occupation Of Borneo

CHAPTER 12..**126**
    The Coast Guard at War, Pacific Landings

ACKNOWLEDGMENTS...**131**

REFERENCES..**134**

INDEX...**135**

TO BE REMEMBERED-IS THE SECRET OF IMMORTALITY!

Map of Borneo 1945

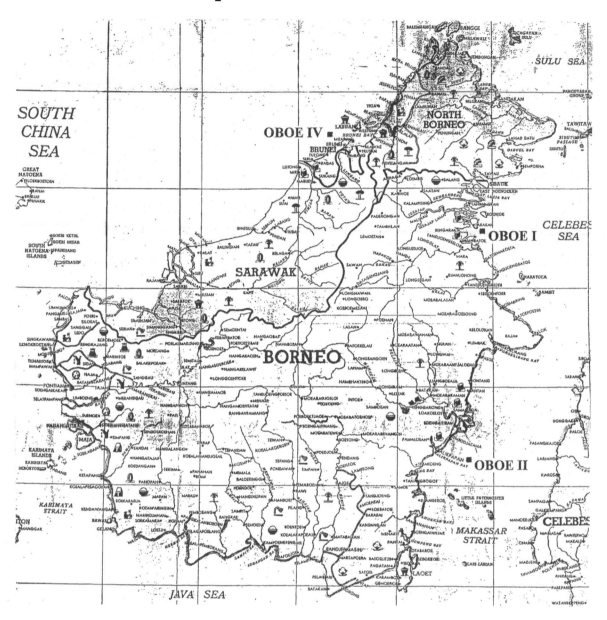

(reprinted from the New York Sunday News, August 5, 1945).
News Map by Staff artist Sundberg

CHAPTER 1
History of the 593rd EB&SR:

The Engineer Special Brigades operated in the Southwest Pacific Theater of Operations for a little over three years during the World War II conflict with the Japanese. First to arrive was the 2nd Brigade who reached New Guinea in the spring of 1943; then came the 3rd Brigade in January 1944; and the 4th Brigade arrived in March 1944. These three brigades made a total of one hundred and forty eight landings during their tour of duty in the Southwest Pacific. Since the 2nd Brigade had a longer tour of combat duty they made a total of eighty six landings; the 3rd Brigade made sixty landings total and the 4th Brigade was credited with two landings.

These three brigades and their attached units earned the Presidential Unit Citation three times; and the Meritorious Unit Plaque five times. Individual amphibious engineers were awarded a Medal of Honor, three Distinguished Service Crosses, sixty nine Silver Stars and more than twelve hundred fifty other combat medals such as the Bronze Star, Soldier's Medal and the Purple Heart.

The landing craft of these three brigades transported as many as four million passengers, placed on shore three million tons of cargo and traveled more than seven million miles during their time in combat. They assembled more than twenty five hundred landing craft. The gunners of the brigades shot down more than fifty Japanese aircraft and a hundred and fifty enemy boats were captured or destroyed. Over one hundred fifty amphibious engineers had been killed in battle by the end of the war.

The 593rd Engineer Boat & Shore Regiments activation was at Camp Edwards, Massachusetts, located on Cape Cod, during the period 6-12 August 1942. This was the time when companies and battalions were being staffed. Incoming troops were given special training and indoctrination programs on amphibious warfare procedures were in the process of being developed.

Colonel Oliver Van den Berg assumed command of the new regiment on 27 August 1942. Officers were assigned from the Amphibious Engineer Command. Enlisted personnel consisted primarily of cadres from Camp Forest, Tennessee; the 186th Field Artillery personnel from Pine Camp, New York; and recruits from Camp Croft, South Carolina;

Fort Bragg, North Carolina; Camp Lee, Virginia; Fort Lewis, Washington; Camp Crowder, Missouri; Fort Leonard Wood, Missouri; Fort McClellan, Alabama; Fort Belvoir, Virginia; and Fort Williams, Maine. A large percentage of enlisted men arriving at the amphibious brigade came through the Special Engineer Amphibian Command recruiting program and many reported without having received basic training.

At Camp Edwards the amphibious personnel were fortunate that exceptional training facilities were provided. The personnel were sent to training schools such as Higgins Boats, Gray Marine and Hall Scott engines, propeller repair, navigation, signal, caterpillar tractor, stevedore, radar, rocket and to the Marine Amphibious Training Center.

On 28 October 1942, the regiment moved, by train, from Camp Edwards to Camp Carrabelle, Florida, and arrived there on 2 November 1942. Soon after arriving, the name of the camp was changed to Camp Gordon Johnston.

In Florida the boat companies practiced every day in the training of the landing craft operation crews, maintenance procedures for boat engines and hulls and in the development of beachhead assaults. Mock amphibious landings were made using the troops of the 28th and 38th Infantry Divisions. It was here during one of these mock landings that the men became aware of the dangers associated with amphibious warfare. On March 1, 1943, the regiment engaged in a practice amphibious beach assault training maneuvers when a hurricane caught the landing craft offshore: loaded with soldiers and equipment. In an attempt to carry out the planned assault landings in the heavy seas and high winds, fourteen soldiers from the infantry units were drowned when they attempted to exit the landing craft at the beach. This disaster taught everyone that weather was to be reckoned with and respected when at sea in small craft.

On 18 April 1943, the regiment moved from Camp Gordon Johnston to the East Garrison area of Fort Ord, California. Prior to its departure from Florida, a number of the men of the regiment formed a provisional boat company which navigated a convoy of thirty landing craft from Florida to Camp Edwards, Massachusetts. This was a noteworthy 1800 mile trip and all boats arrived in good condition. The men of the provisional boat company joined their unit in California after delivering the landing craft to Cape Cod. In mid December 1943, the regiment moved to

Camp Stoneman, California where they prepared for immediate shipment overseas.

On 8 January 1944, the regiment boarded the USAT Sea Flasher at San Francisco and departed for the Southwest Pacific Theater of Operation. The regiment arrived at Goodenough Island, New Guinea on 2 February 1944. From here each of the boat companies moved up to the battle front. First to Lae, then Finschafen, New Guinea; to Arawe, New Britain; then Saidor and Madang, New Guinea; next to Aitape and Hollandia, Maffin Bay, Wakde Island, Biak Island, Noemfoor Island and then to Morotai Island in the Dutch East Indies. From Morotai the boat battalion of the regiment participated in the three Borneo assault operations.

The 593rd Engineer Boat & Shore Regiment departed the United States for the combat war zone of the Southwest Pacific Theater of Operations on 8 January 1944 and arrived at Goodenough Island, some forty miles up the coast of New Guinea from Milne Bay, New Guinea. Transport to the war zone was aboard the United States Army Transport "Sea Flasher", a new Liberty ship and the first troop ship to travel to the Pacific unescorted. The ship's captain had lost his last ship to Japanese submarines off the coast of the Christmas Islands

Upon arrival at Goodenough Island, in a heavy rainstorm, the troops climbed down the rope ladder nets to the awaiting landing craft for transport to the beach. This was to be their first taste of torrential equatorial rain squalls, jungle mud, insects, leeches and a dire feeling of uneasiness for this group of fighting men. No amount of training stateside could have prepared these men of the regiment for the conditions they encountered those first weeks there in the jungles and mud of New Guinea.

New Guinea is an island of the eastern Malay Archipelago just north of Australia. The island is divided into two parts, the western portion belongs to Indonesia and the eastern portion to Papua New Guinea. It is the second largest island in the world, the climate is tropical and the rainfall is over three hundred inches per year making the island one of the wettest places on earth. The central highlands remained undiscovered by the outside world until after World War II.

Goodenough is a forested volcanic island that was occupied by the Japanese for a few months in 1942 and was recaptured some time later by the Allies. At Goodenough the personnel of the regiment became acclimated to the jungle environment and were supplied with landing craft from the boat assembly plant in Milne Bay. The first group to move out proceeded by company landing craft two hundred miles up the coast of New Guinea to Dregger Harbor at Finschafen, where they set up a base camp. From Finschafen one boat company moved to Arawe, New Britain to support troops fighting on the island. This required regular convoy runs from New Guinea to New Britain while other craft of the company handled troops and supply runs up river to the forward fighting units.

The next unit of the regiment to embark on a mission loaded their landing craft aboard the LSD Sheridan and joined an assault convoy and departed for Aitape, New Guinea, near Hollandia. They made the assault landing with the 32nd Infantry Division on the beach. Later this company made landings on Seleo and Ali Islands lying six miles offshore of Aitape. This unit remained here for six months running missions up and down the coast and unloading Liberty ships. On this mission the company lost fourteen landing craft, one officer and five enlisted men.

By the end of March 1944, the third boat company was prepared for its first combat mission. Unit personnel loaded on to company landing craft along with the 5th Australian Division and proceeded up the New Guinea coast to make a surprise assault landing at Saidor, Bogajim and Madang in Papua New Guinea. In rapid succession, landings were made at Alexishafen and along the coast of Hansa Bay. At Madang this company developed special gun boats to provide heavy fire power of rockets and 50 caliber machine gun fire to support landing craft troop and supply missions moving up the rivers. Later this unit moved to Aitape, New Guinea to become a part of the 6th Australian Division who were fighting the enemy in Wewak and the Sepik River area. It was from Aitape that this company moved to Morotai Island to prepare for the Borneo operation.

In June 1944 the company that was in Arawe, New Britain moved up the New Guinea coast to Maffin Bay in Dutch New Guinea. Here they performed lighterage unloading Liberty ships and making supply runs for the Air Corps. Later they moved again, three hundred miles along the coast to Manim Island, a small atoll just off shore of Noemfoor Island. Their next move was to Sansapor at the very northwestern tip of Dutch New Guinea. At this location they maintained a fueling station and performed lighterage, unloading ships. From here the company moved to Morotai Island to prepare for the Borneo operation.

The company that had made the original landing at Aitape, moved up the coast to Noemfoor Island in October 1944. At this location they performed lighterage, provided resupply missions to Biak Island, did river patrols and recon missions around the island. From here they moved to Morotai Island to prepare for the Borneo operation.

The boat companies always worked as separate units attached to Infantry divisions and seldom did they work with each other. These units provided transportation and movement for land based troops. With the lack of roadways on land the easiest way to travel was by boat along the coast and up the rivers. The lack of docks and ports for large vessels made it impossible to unload supplies without small boats for lighterage. The shore companies of the regiment were combat construction engineers who cleared jungle to build roads and airfields, they prepared fuel dumps, built pipelines, constructed buildings and built port facilities. The amphibian engineers filled several important needs of the troops fighting in the jungle environment of New Guinea. They moved troops to the area of the enemy, remained there to support and resupply them and the shore companies provided the facilities needed to support the operations on shore.

The men of the first battalion, 593rd Engineer Boat & Shore Regiment, Third Special Brigade had come a long way from Milne Bay to Sansapor, participating in combat from one end of New Guinea to the other during the past eighteen months. All the boat companies had worked as separate amphibious units since their arrival in the south west Pacific. They were spread along the coast of New Guinea from Aitape to Sansapor when the time came for them to participate in the largest and last amphibious operations of the war, the three OBOE Operations. Each boat company was to be attached to an Australian infantry division in the three amphibious landings designed and planned to retake the Island of Borneo from the Japanese. Each company of the boat battalion was notified to stop operations at their present base and move all personnel and material to Loengee. Loengee Island, a small atoll, a thousand yards off shore of the southern tip of Morotai Island in the Dutch East Indies. This was the staging area for the three OBOE operations in Borneo.

The first company to arrive at the staging area was "B" company and they arrived from Noemfoor Island. They were also the first to depart on a Borneo mission. The company departed Noemfoor Island on 2 April 1945 for Sansapor, they arrived there and refueled and proceeded to the staging area and arriving there on 4 April. The first platoon of company "B" was based at Sansapor and they joined the company on 16 April. When the company arrived at the staging area they immediately commenced preparations to house and feed the remainder of the boat battalion as it arrived on the atoll. "B" companies mission was OBOE ONE, they would participate in the assault landings on Tarakan Island, just off the northeast coast of Borneo.

Headquarters company Boat Battalion was also based at Noemfoor Island when they were notified to present themselves at the staging area. They moved out by company landing craft on 20 April. Their first stop was at Sansapor for fuel and on this leg of the movement they were beset with heavy seas and torrential rains. One landing craft was swamped and sank carrying with it all the company records, fortunately the crew and the other personnel were rescued. This passage from Noemfoor to Sansapor pass close in to the tip of New Guinea which is known as "the bird's head." This area is known for heavy seas and strong cross currents.

Company "A" was next to leave for the staging area. This unit had been based at Noemfoor since October 1944, they had been there long enough to settle in and become comfortable. The company craft were loaded and the convoy departed the island 22 April 1945. They stopped for fuel at Sansapor and proceeded towards the staging area but they almost met disaster in the Halmaheras. The unit navigator got off course and took the convoy to the Halmaheras, an island where the Japanese were still in control. Fortunately the landing craft were intercepted by patrolling Navy PT boats and escorted out of the danger zone. The company arrived at the staging area on 24 April. Upon arrival they immediately commenced to prepare for their part in the OBOE TWO operation.

Company "C" came from Tumeleo Island, an atoll near Aitape, by convoy of company landing craft. On 22 May 1945, the convoy departed for Hollandia and arrived there 24 May. Additional fuel rations and supplies were loaded at Hollandia.

A photograph of the 593rd's tents at Camp Cotuit (on Cape Cod), Massachusetts – or as the men of the 593rd called it: "Camp-can-do it" 1943. Photo courtesy of William Snowman of Company A.

Barracks life at Camp Gordon Johnston (Carrabelle), Florida in 1943. The fellow holding the box of cookies from home and looking directly into the camera is Bill Snowman of Company A. The other fellas are unidentified. Photo courtesy of William Snowman.

Next stop was at Wakde Island, then Biak Island, arriving there 27 May. The only mishap was the loss of two slower craft that got lost during the night but they were located and towed in the following day. The convoy departed Biak on 29 May for Noemfoor Island and arriving there in a heavy downpouring rain and very rough seas. They departed Noemfoor Island 30 May for Sansapor, experiencing heavy rainfall and high seas all the way, refueling and proceeding to the staging area on 3 June 1945.

Camp Gordon Johnston Remembered

Robert Boddy, formerly of Company "C" of the 593rd Engineer Boat & Shore Regiment of the 3rd Engineer Special Brigade during World War II, the Amphibian Engineers. Bob recalls the time that he hunted with grappling hooks for the bodies of his comrades in arms that were drowned in an ill-advised night training exercise.

Sargeant Robert Boddy, in 1943, was a member of the amphibious training group taking part in a training exercise that eventful night. He remembers there was a stiff southeast wind that night and it was whipping up waves as high as he had ever seen in the Gulf of Mexico. Heavy rain squalls lashed at the windows of the landing craft. It was the kind of night that neither man or beast should have ventured out, but the commanding officer gave the order to proceed. Boddy described the weather as a "stinky yellow mess," and you could hardly see your hand before your face. Nevertheless the order was to go! Some twenty to thirty landing craft, each with twenty or more soldiers aboard proceeded into the planned exercise. In addition to the landing craft there were a number of cabin cruisers, taken over by the army for training and these smaller boats took the brunt of the storm.

The commanding officer, perhaps a bit nervous, called Washington for an official go ahead and the officials in Washington said the weather was okay and that the exercise should proceed. No one knew for sure if the call was placed to Washington.

The task force took off from Alligator Point, which lay along the coast about six miles northeast of Carrabelle, Florida. Due to the increasing intensity of the storm, they rendezvoused for some time out in the bay, hoping the storm would subside. As nightfall approached the storm worsened but they were ordered to go on with the mission. There was such poor visibility and such strong winds and rough water that none of the craft knew for certain where they were located in comparison as to where they were ordered to land the troops. All the craft headed for the beach and a safe haven. Some including Boddy, who were experienced seamen, took off to go around Dog Island hoping to reach safety in the big Carrabelle river. Soon after they rounded Dog Island, Boddy's boat began to founder. In the dark, with pressing navigation problems and wearing bulky rain gear he hadn't noticed the large amount of water that had accumulated in the boat. On inspection he found that the sand traps had filled up, making the pumps inoperable. He and all of his crew were violently seasick and realizing his problems he almost panicked. He yelled at his men to get busy and clean the traps if they wanted to live. They did, and they finally reached the mouth of the river. Several of the other craft had already reached a safe haven in the river before they arrived. By Sunday morning the storm had abated. With its end came the grisly task of grappling for the bodies of those that had drowned during the night. He estimates that they found between thirty and forty bodies. All the soldiers were wearing life belts equipped with CO_2 cartridges, and what Boddy doesn't understand until this day is why the soldiers had not inflated them, all it took to inflate them was one squeeze. Boddy thinks the landing craft must have struck a sand bar and the soldiers disembarked thinking they were on the beach and stepped into deep water and drowned.

In later years, in late November, right after hurricane Kate, a woman strolling the beach near Lanark discovered a set of dog tags that were half buried in the sand. Whether they are from that fateful night in 1943, is not yet known. For the time being it is one more poignant incident in the saga of Camp Gordon Johnston.

Sargeant Boddy left Camp Gordon Johnston around Easter in 1943, on his way to overseas duty in the Southwest Pacific Theater of Operation.

This story is an excerpt from Company C's reunion booklet of August 1987 at Bloomington, Minnesota. The book was prepared by the survivors of Charlie company, 593rd EB&SR, for Robert Boddy, Lawrence Taylor and Welton Stein.

Medals Award Ceremony
Cp. San Luis Obispo, Cal.

Left to right: Regimental Commander, Colonel Keyes; a Lieutenant (Gen. Ogden's aide) name not known; behind the Lieutenant and whose face is covered by the Lt's head, Lt. Brim; next to him, 1st Sgt. Crow; General Ogden pinning the Bronze Star on Lt. James A. pounds (one of the authors of this book): Master Sgt. Wilkinson and Lieutenant Colonel Motto. Photo courtesy of Jim Pounds.

Douglas MacArthur

Commander in Chief
Southwest Pacific

General of the Army, Douglas MacArthur, with his Chief of Staff, Lt. Gen. Richard E. Sutherland (left) and the 5th Army's Commander, Lt. Robert L. Eichelberger. U.S. Army Signal Corps. Photo reprinted from "Surf and Sand," 1945. Courtesy of Julius Grossberg.

Landing Craft Mechanized (LCM)

A typical LCM (this particular one was from Company "C"). Frank Simmons was the Engineman on this boat. Photo courtesy of Mary Simmons, Frank's Widow.

The Landing craft were fifty and fifty six feet in length. Maximum beam twelve feet amidship, flat bottomed and capable of carrying a net payload of fifty tons. The bow consisted of a large ramp extending the full width of the craft, it being lowered by a winch and cables and sealed to the craft's gunwales in the raised position with a large rubber gasket to prevent the craft from filling with water when loaded and underway in heavy seas. The aft ten feet of the LCM contained the engine room, the wheel house, ramp operating winch, fuel tanks and two General Motors "Jimmie" diesel engines. Built into the gunwales and double bottoms, there were twelve sealed air flotation tanks. These tanks made it impossible to sink the LCM completely unless it were fully loaded. The construction was all welded one quarter inch steel plate.

The design purpose was for transporting large vehicles, six by six trucks, tanks and small trucks and jeeps. Two jeeps fit nicely in the cargo bay. The LCM could be run up on the beach, the ramp lowered and the vehicles backed in to the cargo by, the ramp raised, the boat would back off the beach and the payload was on its way. In addition the LCMs were used extensively for lightering cargo from Liberty ships anchored off shore to the beachheads. This was the work the boat crews disliked the most, for it went on night and day, without relief when the ships were being unloaded.

The crew of the LCMs consisted of three men, a Coxswain with a rate of Tec/4, an engineman with the rate of Tec/5 and a seaman rated Private First Class. When the boats worked around the clock, as they did many times in the assault operations, one man slept and two men were on duty at all times, each having eight hours duty out of twenty four.

Living and working aboard the LCMs was tough, cramped quarters, limited storage for extra dry clothing and food and poor facilities for bathing, laundry and shaving (if you still had a razor). Most crews built a large cover over the wheelhouse, this served to keep most of the direct rays of the tropical sun from cooking their nose, ears, face and arms. It also served as a shelter from the seemingly constant monsoon rains. During the season, it would rain in the morning, let up for a few hours and rain again in the afternoon and rain again at night. The crews would build frames over the rear eight feet of the cargo well and cover it with canvas. This arrangement made a place to put bunks and stow their gear. Some men stored their personal things in one of the flotation tanks in the cargo well. Food was warmed on the exhaust manifolds in the engine room, Water for coffee and bouillon was also heated on the manifolds.

Maintenance of the LCMs was a big problem, operating as they did around the coral reefs and landing on the coral and lava sand beaches, bent propellers were a constant problem."

Brigadier General David D. Ogden, Commander of the 3rd Engineer Special Brigade, at the wheel of an LCVP. Reprinted from "Surf and Sand," the saga of the 533rd Engineer Boat and Shore Regiment and the 1461st. Engineer Maintenance Company. 1942-1945. Photo courtesy of Julius Grossberg.

Brigadier General David A.D. (Dad) Ogden

Colonel Ogden assumed command of the Third Engineer Amphibian Brigade (EAR) at Camp Edwards, Massachusetts at the time the brigade was formed on 8 August 1942. He was soon promoted to Brigadier General. He was an excellent commander and commenced a vigorous training program for the unit personnel immediately on assuming command. The General believed in personally directing many of his training plans and the practice maneuvers that were conducted stateside. He was no stranger to his troops and was always there to commend them for a job well done and also to remind them when things went awry.

Overseas he was a capable combat commander and was always in the thick of the fight when one of his units was engaged in battle. There is a story about the time one of his boat units went into Cape Gloucester, New Britain. Due to inclement weather the Air Corps was unable to bomb and strafe the beachhead prior to the landing. The General took off in a Piper L-4 Recon loaded with grenades and dropped the grenades on likely enemy positions.

May 1945, General Ogden was named Area Engineer of the Batangas area of the Philippines.

He directed a construction program to build petroleum dumps, roads, bomb revetments and a hospital. In December 1945, he organized and directed a Service Command on the Japanese Island of Kyushu.

After the war he was given the command of the 2nd Engineer Amphibious Brigade. This brigade was designated as part of the permanent regular peace time army. When war broke out in South Korea, the 2nd was one of the first units to see action in the Korean Conflict.

8

Lieutenant General Eichelberger and Brigadier General Byers (Chief of Staff of the 1st Corps.) upon their arrival from Hollandia, New Guinea, for an inspection of Japanese caves and fortifications on Biak island, New Guinea. They also toured 186th Regimental defenses near Mokmer Drome. U.S. Army Signal Corps. Photographer: Dickerman. Photo courtesy of the National Archives SC14398.

General Robert L. Eichelberger

General Eichelberger, a 1909 graduate of the West Point Military Academy at West Point, New York. He was later the Superintendent of the West Point Military Academy from 1940-1942.

As a member of General MacArthur's Staff, in the Pacific during World War II, he proved himself to be a most capable leader and tactician. It was through his leadership that the American Forces won their first battle in New Guinea in the recapture of Buna on the southeast coast of Papua New Guinea. He directed the military operations up the coast of New Guinea and the attacks on the Island of New Britain. In September of 1944, he accepted command of the newly formed 8th Army at Hollandia, Dutch New Guinea.

In 1945, he began the recapture of the Philippine Islands. After the Japanese surrender in August 1945, he began the occupation of the Japanese homeland. For three years he directed the Army of Occupation in Japan.

In 1948, he retired from the army and published his memoirs, "Our Jungle Road To Tokyo."

CHAPTER 2
Those Who Served

This chapter features pictures of military personnel and a native civilian, who took part in the assault operations in Bornco during World War II. The soldiers were members of the Boat Battalion of the 593rd Engineer boat & Shore Regiment of the 3rd Engineer Special Brigade with attached Special Support groups and the Australian Army troops who fought on the ground in Borneo.

Harris bin Mohamed Salleh was a young man who was living on Labuan Island, British North Borneo during the Japanese occupation of this island and he witnessed the harsh treatment of the indigenous people of that portion of Borneo by the Japanese Army.

Stella Faye Jordan was an Australian Army nurse who tended the wounded and dying Allied soldiers, Australian and American. Her story tells of how the prisoners of the Japanese Army were treated. She has also provided us with a modern day look at Labuan Island and North Borneo and how they have changed dramatically since the war years.

Bill Roemlein was a member of an air crew of a B-24 liberator Bomber of the 307th Heavy Bomber Group that performed many bomb runs over the beachhead areas where assault landings were to be made. It was this "softening up" by the bombers that saved many amphib and Aussie lives by destroying gun positions, beach obstacles and by destroying the enemy's resources for effective warfare against the assault invasions.

All the other soldiers were of the 593rd Engineer Boat & Shore Regiment and one soldier, Julius Grossberg, was from the 533rd Engineer Boat & Shore Regiment. All these soldiers were either involved in the war against Japanese during World War II in New Guinea or in combat on the Island of Borneo.

Photograph of two Australian soldiers. This photo was taken in Jerusalem on June 11, 1941 and has J. Phil O'Brien (left) and his buddy, Dick Pickup (right). Phil later served on Borneo as many of the Australian soldiers did who served in the Holy Land. Photo courtesy of J. Phil O'Brien.

Loren W. Aicher
Tec 5-Company A
(1922-2003)

Robert L. Anderson
Tec 4- Hq. & Hq
(1921-1997)

Richard W. Alf
Pfc-Company A

Vincent Angeloni
Tec 5-Company B

Hoket V. Ayscue
Tec 5- Company C

Herbert J. Baker
S/Sgt.- Company B

Russell A. Bergeron
Tec 5- Company C

Grover S. Black
S/Sgt.- Company A
(1920 - 2000)

Robert Boddy
Tec 4- Company C

Dwaine Burke
S/Sgt. - Company A
(1921 - 2003)

Donato Caparella
T/Sgt.- Company B

Mario Caporiccio
Capt.- 593rd EBSR
(1914-1999)

Joseph Ciccomoscolo
Pfc- Company B
(1924-1991)

John Cunningham
1st Lt.- Company B
(1921 - 2004)

Chester David and his wife
Marge. Tec 4- Company B

Anthony DeBlasie
T/Sgt.- Company B
(1920 - 2001)

Joseph Davis (standing next to the Jeep).
Driver: Gordon; kneeling left to right: Triola
and Healy. Joe was a Tec 4 in Company A.
(1908-1984).

Albert A. Deprete (left)
with his buddy Danny
Caparella.
Tec 5- Company B
(1922-1953)

Joseph Foeller
T/Sgt.- Company B

Thomas B. Ford
Staff Sgt. Australian Army

William R. Graham
S/Sgt. - Company B

Armand A. Gosselin
Tec 4- Company C
(1915-1996)

Julius Grossberg
Tec- 5 -533rd EBSR
Soldier's medal

Floyd Habermehl
Tec 3- Company A

Michael Harmon
Tec 4- Company C

Albert Herman
Tec 5- Company B

James P. Igoe
Pvt.- Company A
(1923-1999)

Stella Faye Jordan
Cpl.- Australian Nurse

Sampson Judah
Tec 4- Company C

Harold Killoran (left) with his
buddy, Chet Sullivan
Tec 4- Company C
(1921-1990)

Victor Krueger
Tec 5- Company B

Wilmer Laufmann
S/Sgt. - 593rd EBSR

Joseph Lit
Tec 4- Company C

Richard Ledwith
Tec 5- Company A

Lewis Lindsey
T/Sgt. - Company C

Walter P. McMurchy
Tec 5- Company B

Pervis Meaux
Tec 4- Company C

William Medvec
Pfc- Company C

James Merrill
T/Sgt.- Company C

Nathan Michelson
Tec 5- Company B

Edmund Mieszkowski
Tec 5- Company A

Leroy Muschinske (left) with
his life-long friend, Bill Wobeck.
Tec 4-Hq. Co. Boat Battalion

Phillip James O'Brien
Cpl. Australian Army

Herbert Naish
1st Lt. 593rd EBSR
(1909-1997)

J. Carroll Naish (left) and his brother, Herbert Naish (right),
pose with the star of the movie, Gary Cooper (center) on the
set of "Beau Geste," 1939. Both Naish brothers are in the
film. (Courtesy of Mary Naish, Herb's widow).

Deward L. Offutt
S/Sgt. - Company B

John G. Orr and his wife, Ruth
2nd Lt.- Company B

Ernest W. Paquette
Tec 5- Company B

Anton J. Pakiz
Tec 5- Company C

Henry R. Payne
Cpl.- Company A

Epifanio Perez
Tec 5- Company B

James Pullen
Tec-4- Company C
(1917-1997)

Charles Phister
Tec 3- Company C
(1909-1995)

Donald Reddin
Tec 5- Company B
(1920-2000)

Bennie Quigg
Tec 5- Company B

William Roemlein
S/Sgt. 322nd Bomb Sq.

Willis Siegfried
Tec 5- Company A

Frank Simmons
Tec 5- Company C
(1906-1988)

William B. Smith
S/Sgt.- Company B

Frank S. Snars
S/Sgt. Australian Army

John Stauthammer
S/Sgt.- Company C

Welton Stein
Tec 4- Company C

John T. Thompson
Tec 4- Company B

George R. Tregembo
Sgt. 17th Reconn. Sq. US
Army A.F.

Anthony W. Tozzi
S/Sgt.- Company B (1917-1972)
Soldier's Medal

Harris Bin Mohamed Salleh
was a 10 year old boy on
Labuan Island when the
Japanese controlled Borneo

Arthur Verser &
his wife, Adelia
Tec 5- Company A

George Wander
Tec 5- Company C

Jerry Wagner
Tec 5- Company A

Marius Waldman
Tec 5- Company B

Garfield O. Williams
1st Lieut. Company A

CHAPTER 3

AUSTRALIANS ON BORNEO

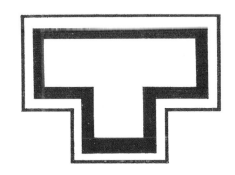

9th Australian Division

TARAKAN ISLAND

Tarakan Island, Borneo, April 30, 1945. Engineers of the 2/13th Field Company, Royal Australian Engineers, on a ruined pipeline jetty after working waist deep in mud and slime to breach wire entanglements for the Infantry invasion. Identified personnel are: (1) Sapper R.A.E. Stevenson; (2) Sapper P. Carroll; (3) Cpl. R.C. Mace; (4) Sapper J.S. Proctor; (5) Sapper G.E. Maxwell; (6) Sapper A.J. Clydesdale; (7) Sapper E.S. Slee (later killed in action at Djoeta-north of the airdrome on Tarakan) and (8) unknown. AWM090915. Photograph is a gift from Dr. Peter Stanley of Canberra, Australia.

Tarakan Island, Borneo, June 21, 1945. Members of a patrol from C Company, 2/24th Infantry Battalion moving along the bed of a small creek on their way to hill 90, via Maple Feature, where they expect to contact 2/4th Commando Squadron. AWM109981. Photograph is a gift from Dr. Peter Stanley of Canberra, Australia.

Tarakan Island, Borneo, May 1, 1945. LSTs beached, pontoons erected and unloading in progress during the Allied Invasion of the Island. AWM28276. Photograph is a gift from Dr. Peter Stanley of Canberra, Australia.

BRUNEI BAY *LABUAN & MUARA ISLANDS:*

Troops from the 24th Brigade, 9th Australian Division land on Labuan Island. Photography by the U.S. Army Signal Corps. Photo courtesy of the National Archives SC-266487.

Australian soldiers return from investigating a house used by the Japanese for a headquarters. No sniper opposition in this section of Brunei, Borneo, Netherlands East Indies. U.S. Army Signal Corps. photograph. Photographer: Williams. August 8, 1945. Photo courtesy of the National Archives SC266415.

Troops from the 24th Brigade Hq., 9th Australian Division, moving up from beach after making a landing on Labuan Island, Borneo. Photograph by U.S. Army Signal Corps. Photographer: Heller. Photo courtesy of the National Archives SC266408.

Aussie engineers remove aerial bombs used as anti-vehicular mines on a road south of Brunei, North Borneo. In hurried retreat, the Japanese forgot to fuse the bombs. Photograph by U.S. Army Signal Corps. Photographer: Williams. Photo courtesy of the National Archives SC266435.

Men of the 24th Brigade, 9th Australian Division, wading ashore during landings on Labuan Island, Borneo. Photograph by U.S. Army Signal Corps. Photographer: Heller. Photo courtesy of the National Archives SC266403.

Australian soldiers crossing hastily repaired section of a Red Beach jetty accidentally hit in the initial bombardment. Red Beach on Muara Island, Brunei Bay, Borneo, N.E.I. Photograph by U.S. Army Signal Corps. Photographer: Williams. Photo courtesy of the National Archives SC266414.

Men of the 24th Brigade, 9th Australian Division, wading ashore from LCIs during landing on Labuan Island. Photograph by U.S. Army Signal Corps. Photographer: Heller. June 10, 1945. Photo courtesy of the National Archives SC266402.

Troops of the 24th Brigade, 9th Australian Division, coming on shore during landing on Labuan Island, Brunei Bay, Borneo. Photograph by U.S. Army Signal Corps. Photographer: Heller. Photo courtesy of the National Archives SC211811.

Australian engineers removing bombs from the road to Brunei, Borneo, Netherlands East Indies, June 11, 1945. Photograph by U.S. Army Signal Corps. Photographer: Williams. Photo courtesy of the National Archives SC168222.

S troops 2/11th Commando Squadron of the 24th Brigade on the edge of the perimeter brewing tea. Labuan Island, Brunei Bay, Borneo. Photograph by U.S. Army Signal Corps. Photographer: Heller. August 7, 1945. Photo courtesy of the National Archives SC266412.

Bren gun position of the 24th Brigade on perimeter a mile beyond. Labuan Island, Brunei Bay, Borneo. Photograph by U.S. Army Signal Corps. Photographer: Heller. August 7, 1945. Photo courtesy of the National Archives SC266410.

BALIKPAPAN

Australian troops gather in front of partially destroyed Japanese beach defense position and radio station at Balikpapan, Borneo. Photograph by U.S. Army Signal Corps. Photographer: Haas. August 23, 1945. Photo courtesy of the National Archives SC19728.

Aussies of the 18th Brigade, 7th Division, 2nd of the 10th Battalion, passing by a pill-box set on fire by Aussie tanks, as they enter the town of Balikpapan on Borneo. Photograph by U.S. Army Signal Corps. Photographer: Murphy. Photo courtesy of the National Archives SC266426.

Aussies of the 18th Brigade, 7th Division, 2nd of the 10th Battalion, passing by a pill-box set on fire by Aussie tanks, as they enter the town of Balikpapan on Borneo. Photograph by U.S. Army Signal Corps. Photographer: Murphy. Photo courtesy of the National Archives SC266427.

Bren gun team of the 18th Brigade, 7th Division, takes cover from machine gun fire during Aussies' advance into Balikpapan, Borneo. Photograph by U.S. Army Signal Corps. Photographer: Lt. Novak. Photo courtesy of the National Archives SC266433.

Men of the 18th Brigade, 7th Australian Division approach cautiously a Japanese tunnel under hill 87 at Balikpapan, Borneo. Photograph by U.S. Army Signal Corps. Photographer: Lt. Novak. Photo courtesy of the National Archives SC266425.

Australians in action!

Machine gunner lets go with a burst at a suspected Japanese position in their advance through Dutch Barracks (1st Australian Corp.; 18th Brigade; 7th Division, Company C). July 2, 1945. Photographer: Haas. Photo courtesy of the National Archives SC266423.

Aussies of the 18th Brigade, 2nd of the 4th Field Regiment, use 25 pound shells as they shell enemy positions 5,700 yards away. Borneo. Photograph by U.S. Army Signal Corps. Photographer: Murphy. Photo courtesy of the National Archives SC266420.

Troops of the 24th Battalion, Australian, cross a culvert on the road to Tarakan, Borneo. Photographer: Klein. May 5, 1945. Photo released for publication, Bureau of Public Relations, War Department, Washington, D.C. Photo courtesy of the National Archives SC266409.

Tanks and troops of the 24th Aussie Brigade advance after encountering no opposition to landing on Labuan Island, Borneo. June 10, 1945. Released by the War Department, Washington, D.C. Photographer: Rothberg. Photo courtesy of the National Archives SC266406.

Infantry start advance through wrecked barracks (1st Australian Corps; 7th Division, 18th Brigade, Company C) on Balikpapan, Borneo. Photographer: Haas. Photo courtesy of the National Archives SC266421.

Australians of the 25th Brigade, 2nd of the 31st Infantry Battalion, 7th Division, wait on beach before moving up to the front, just after unloading from an LCM, Borneo, August 29, 1945. Photograph by U.S. Army Signal Corps. Photographer: Murphy. Photo courtesy of the National Archives SC266422.

A Japanese pill-box on Tarakan Island, Borneo. Note one of the Aussies' rifles sticking out of the slit, just for the photo. Photo courtesy of Thomas B. Ford, Queensland, Australia.

One of the Australian tanks that got knocked out when it ran over a mine (a 250k bomb). Photo courtesy of Thomas B. Ford, Queensland, Australia.

CHAPTER 4
The Bombing Of Borneo

Reprinted from "We'll Say Goodbye." (The story of the "Long Rangers") The 307th Bombardment Group (HV) of the 13th Army Air Force, 1945.

Strikes flown from Morotai against installations at Borneo form one of the most varied and colorful periods in our history. The targets attacked called for the use of everything in the "Book for Bombing with the B-24," including a couple of chapters that were dictated extemporaneously, so to speak, and very much on the spot: There was the time; for instance, when a lone Liberator made an attack on a Japanese ship off the northwest coast of Borneo, and missed. One bomb had hung up, however, and when repeated runs over the target still proved unsuccessful, a stunt was resorted to that made bombardiering history. The co-pilot stood on his seat to get a clear view of the vessel under attack, and, at a hand signal from him, relayed by the navigator who was standing in the forward part of the bomb bays, the bombardier pried the recalcitrant bomb loose with a screw driver and scored a direct hit, sending another ship to the bottom to join the ever increasing Japanese undersea fleet.

The Japanese, having lost one of their north-south shipping routes when the Celebes came within short range of Allied air power, moved west to the second of their three main lanes, the one passing the Macassar Straits. This rapidly developed into a happy hunting ground for B-24s of the "Long Rangers." Shipping sweeps through the Macassar Straits and along the east coast of Borneo soon made this area such a danger zone for the Nips' shipping that again they were forced to move west, this time utilizing their last remaining route, that through the China sea. Shipping, however, wasn't the only target bombed by Liberators from the 307th in the Borneo region. A systematic destruction of the dozen Jap airfields that ringed the northeast and northwest coasts of Borneo was also undertaken and enemy strips from Miri on the west coast to Sepinggan on the east coast were "Rangerized" and finally catalogued in the unserviceable column. This served the dual purpose of not only preparing Borneo for its final conquest by Allied forces but also protected the flank of Allied shipping moving up through the Sulu Sea enroute to the landings at Mindoro and Luzon.

Oil installations also came in for their share of attention during this period of our history. In addition to the Borneo oil fields at Balikpapan, the Japs were also working fields at Miri, Tarakan and Sanga Sanga. Although very secondary in comparison to the production of Balikpapan, still they contributed a vital ingredient for the total Jap economy and thus fell heir to the hammer blows that Allied air power was delivering to all targets it could reach. Mass raids were directed against Miri and Tarakan, and individual strikes were flown against those two targets as well as Sanga Sanga. These individual missions and lone shipping prowls formed the background for some of the most spectacular efforts in the history of the group.

Take, for example, the lone B-24 that dropped its string of bombs through the oil tanks at Lutong Refinery at Miri and then made repeated low level strafing passes despite accurate, intense AA fire that sieved the plane and wounded two of the crew members. When this destruction-bent pilot and his equally rapacious crew finally left the scene of action they had destroyed, single handedly, a goodly part of the Nips' oil installations in the area and left blazing fires with columns of smoke visible for many miles. This one attack practically wiped Lutong off the list of worth while targets. *Note:* SABU Dastigar, who played the "Elephant Boy" in the movies in the 1930s, and who was born in India, became a U.S. Citizen on January 4, 1943, the very same day that he had joined the U.S. Army Air Force to fight the Japanese during World War II. Sabu became a nose-turret gunner on a B-24 Liberator bomber of the 307th Bomb Group (HV), the "Long Rangers." He received the Air Medal (with four clusters) and the Distinguished Flying Cross for his actions in the Southwest Pacific over Borneo and other sites. Sabu was a fine actor, but after the war had ended in 1945, fewer parts were available in Hollywood movies for an East Indian-American actor. His last two movies in Hollywood were *Black Narcissus* in 1946, and *A Tiger Walks*, released in 1964, which was his final appearance. Sabu died of a heart attack after finishing that movie in 1963. He was only 39 years old when he died. Sabu was in the same outfit on B-24 bombers as was Bill Roemlein. Bill also mentioned to the authors of *Operation Borneo* that the actor John Payne was also in the 307th Bomb Group during World War II. (See page 51 for photograph).

Strategic conference of the aircrew of the 307th B-24 Liberator bomber group before taking off for operations, in the air over Borneo.

A B-24 Liberator bomber dropping bombs over its target. Photo courtesy of Bill Roemlein.

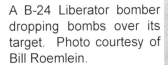

Exploding storage tank throws a sheet of flame into the air as Japanese oil refinery at Tarakan, Borneo is blasted.

Remembrances of Bill Roemlein, S/Sgt. USAAF.

We began putting together a B-24 Bomber crew in late May 1944 when we all first met at March Air Force Base, Riverside, California. There were two pilots, one from Indiana and the other from Texas, one navigator from Ohio and one bombardier from Iowa. The six gunners were from New Jersey, New York, Washington, Pennsylvania and Arkansas. Each member of the crew had recently completed his training, i.e. mechanics, communications, gunnery and so forth.

The training flights took us all over southern California, Nevada, Utah, Arizona and there were many over water flights. We continually practiced precision bombing, aerial targets, emergency landings and we sharpened our individual skills. Upon completion we were assigned a new B-24 which we flew to Hamilton Field, California, located just north of San Francisco, in September 1944. After a short four day leave we departed for Hawaii. It was sad and dramatic flying over the Golden Gate Bridge and heading for the unknown.

Our combat mission started with our first stop at Guadalcanal. For the first two weeks we flew practice and search and rescue missions. From here we moved to Lae, New Guinea where we started our string of 40 missions. Our 307th Heavy Bomber Squadron flew from many staging areas such as Wewak and Hollandia. As General MacArthur's army units, along with the valiant Australian army captured various Japanese strongholds, we continued moving on. Once a new base was secured, our very efficient Naval Sea Bees quickly constructed runways to accommodate B-24s plus fighter planes. Living conditions were very severe, hot, high humidity, malaria and C-rations. These conditions plus dense jungle made for some very unhappy warriors.

February 1945 brought us to our final move to the island of Morotai in the Dutch East Indies. Since we stayed here for the remainder of our missions, life became less intolerable. Upon completing our 25th mission we were granted a ten day leave to Sydney, Australia. (see page 137).

Returning from Australian leave we commenced to hit many Philippine targets including Corregidor, Cavite, Clark Field and Manila. Other targets were the oil refinery at Balikpapan, Borneo, Java, Sumatra and various targets in the Dutch East Indies.

A typical mission day started with the wake up call at 05:00 hours, breakfast, briefing and crew orientation until 06:15 hours and then off to the airstrip. Each member checked his equipment Take off at 07:00 hours. Most targets required from two to four hours flying time with a round trip from four to eight hours. Over target, suspense was very high, fighters, flak and etc. Once the bombs were dropped the pilot would clear the area very quickly. The trip back to base and lunch which was usually Spam, canned fruit and a smoke. Many cigarettes were smoked to relieve the tension. Upon seeing home base many prayers were said that we were home safe. We then went through debriefing and were given a shot of rye. We had made one more mission towards the "golden 40."

The early missions, during the battle of the Coral Sea, there was tremendous Japanese fighter activity and unbelievable flak from Japanese warships. The flights over the heavily opposed areas of Java, Sumatra, Borneo and Luzon in the Philippines were memorable.

Being briefed on flights over Borneo, we were told if knocked down, consider the pill, as Borneo was loaded with headhunters. We remembered how it felt to be forced down on Palawan Island in the South China sea after taking many hits. Many times we prayed that the overloaded plane would get off the ground. Bombing the Borneo oil fields at moderately low altitudes was scary. Seeing severe fires climbing high into the sky, we sometimes sensed they would envelope our plane and the crew. Attending-burial services for our fallen comrades was always hard. I remember returning from a mission on my 20th birthday, March 10, 1945, we flew over and observed the invasion of Zamboango, Southern Philippines, it was very impressive. The Australians were a very gracious and friendly people. During our Sydney leave there were superb steaks, beer and girls.

Finally we developed a feeling of disgust and utter hatred for the Japs as they burned the beautiful city of Manila in the Philippines. At long last the war was over and we boarded a troop ship, with Marines and Army personnel for the trip back home to the USA. We landed at San Pedro, California with tears in our eyes, we were so happy to be home again.

ENTERTAINING THE TROOPS

Kay Kyser, his orchestra and Ginny Sims entertaining troops in the Philippine Islands, 1944. Photo courtesy of George Tregembo.

"Thanks For The Memory"

U.S.O. Camp Shows gave us Bob Hope, and we laughed. He and his gang put on the best shows that we had seen. Thanks, Bob.

One of the few bright spots, in fact, the only one of our stay at Wakde, was the Bob Hope show consisting of Bob himself, Frances Langford, Patty Thomas, Jerry Colonna and Tony Romano. (A surprise of the show was the guest appearance of Captain Lanny Ross, a popular singer entertainer of the 40s.) This was the one that we really sweated out, not only was it three hours late, but the temperature must have been well over the century mark. However, the moment Bob walked on the stage with that famous sun helmet and cane and said, I love this beautiful island, with its magnificent palm trees, two of them with tops; all the heat and discomfort was forgotten. When Patty Thomas danced on in that black and red costume (now we knew what we were fighting for) the heat started all over again. She was the loveliest creature we had seen in a long time and she really made a hit. From anyone but Hope, she would have stolen the show; but they don't steal shows from him. He joked with Frances and Patty, he joked alone, he sang in the trio with Jerry Colonna and Tony Romano, he kidded us, he kidded the others in the show, and he kidded himself.

When Frances sang we thought of home, when Patty danced, we thought of all those lovely chicks back there. But when Bob came on we forgot everything and just laughed.

37

Reprinted from "We'll Say Goodbye" (The story of the "Long Rangers" –307th Bombardment Group (VH) of the 13th Army Air Force. 1945.) Art Directors: Fred J. Kaplan and Murray McKeehan. Courtesy of Bill Roemlein.

Iva Togori, a.k.a. Tokyo Rose, captured after the war ended in 1945. She spent some time in jail.

☆ Tokyo Rose

Tokyo Rose, c/o Radio Tokyo (Somewhere in What's Left of Japan).

We've been listening to your line ever since you've been on the air. At times it was the best entertainment we could get. We don't know who you really are, what you look like, or where you get all those American records, but each of us has his own ideas.

With your sexy, silky soft-talk; a couple of innocent-looking syllables, a suggestive whisper, your microphone manner was something new to us. Your rumors, your melodramas of our girls taking to the primrose path, the 4-F'ers taking over, your descriptions of homey scenes, of chicken dinners, of moonlight strolls, of sodas at the corner drug, of petting in the park; your reproductions of beer parlors, pool rooms, of dancing to Glenn Miller, Dorsey, Goodman, Kyser. You flashed flickers of home, you talked across the breakfast table,

you gave out with gossip; you were intimate, love-purring, cooing. That was your line, your technique. Why, you had a patent on it! And through all this chit-chat you played, your old scratchy, corny records you brought over from the States.

"The Rose" has become a legend, a South Pacific yarn: Over our beers, in years to come, we will talk of you and smile and try to figure out just what kind of a gal you were. You were a part of our jungle life, a tropical whiff of amusement. Your program was always good for a laugh!

With all your subtle propaganda trying to scare us or make us homesick, you, in fact, gave us some of the most entertaining programs we had till we got our own Jungle Network going with a taste of our real, present-day America. For a while you were our only program with a flavor of home: You filled the gap of loneliness, and we liked you. So orchids to you and thanks for the memories.

CHAPTER 5
The Tarakan Invasion

Plans for the defeat of the Japanese on Borneo Island were being considered as early as March 1945. The island had been occupied by the Japanese in December 1941 and early 1942. Their main purpose was the exploitation of oil in the southern and eastern areas and the rubber to support their war machines. A move against the enemy on this island would deny them a ready source of these two vital resources.

The Montclair Plan for the liberation of Borneo, as planned by General Headquarters, Southwest Pacific Area called for the use of Australian and Netherlands ground troops in the initial assaults. Support troops would include United States and Australian naval and air forces.

Tarakan Island off the northeast coast of Borneo was chosen as the initial assault area and the operation was code named OBOE I. Planning was commenced on 14 March and operation instructions were issued on 21 March 1945.

When orders were received from GHQ, SWPA for the assignment of an engineer amphibious company for OBOE I, the regimental commander designated "B" company, supported by one platoon of the 1463rd Engineer Maintenance company and a small medical detachment for the task. At the planning conferences held at Morotai, all details of the "B" company's duties in the operation were discussed with all the participating forces. Due to mud in the designated beaching areas, the Australian Brigade Commander decided the LCMs would transport the most essential tanks and doziers ashore.

This assault on Tarakan was originally planned for 29 April 1945, but after further investigation of tides, in the proposed beaching areas, it was found that the highest tide of the year would occur on 1 May. The 26th Brigade Commander changed D-day to 1 May and the change was approved by GHQ, AFPAC. All planning and orientation was completed prior to 27 April. The assault convoy proceeded from Morotai, on 27 April 1945.

"B" company's personnel, supplies, material and landing craft were loaded aboard or were towed by the naval craft to the Task Force. An LSD loaded two "J" boats and 17 LCMs. Twenty two other LCMs were deck loaded on ships or towed by LSTs. All towed craft were loaded with cargo. There were to be

a total of thirty nine LCMs, eighteen of which would take part in the initial assault on the beachheads.

The manifest of the ship, AKA USS Titania, showed eight LCMs deck loaded (M-9-B-36, 37, 41, 45, 43, 38, 49 and 40), and a compliment of "B" company personnel of one officer and 35 enlisted men.

HMAS Monoora carried two LCMs deck loaded (M-9-B-7 and 15), with a compliment of three officers and ten enlisted men.

HMAS Westralia carried two LCMs deck loaded (M-9-B-4 and 5), and a compliment of nine enlisted men.

Nine LCMs were towed by LSTs, (M-9-B-2, 21,8, 44,14,11,, 9,12, and 3) these LCMs carried a compliment of one officer and 59 enlisted men.

The fifth assault wave on Red Beach Two contained five LCMs (M-9-B-18, 20, 29, 26 and 22), and personnel on these landing craft consisted of one officer and eighty one enlisted men.

LCMs from the LSD Rushmore, consisted of two LCMs (M-9, B-19 and 27) and thirty eight enlisted men and these two craft went into Green Beach. One in the fifth wave. Three LCMs (M-9-B-17, 28, and 23) with three officers and forty nine enlisted men landed in the fifth wave on Green Beach Two. Six LCMs (M-9-B-34,24,25,35,33, and 32) with one officer and sixty one enlisted men landed in the sixth wave. There were boats that were not in the initial waves, two "J" boats, one maintenance boat and one LCM (M-9-B-6) with a compliment of twelve enlisted men.

The OBOE I task force arrived offshore of the designated beaches on Tarakan Island at 05:30 hours on D-day 1 May 1945. The assault waves lined up one and a half miles offshore in their designated order and in wave formation. The naval bombardment of the beach areas began sharply at 07:15 hours and this was followed by air strikes. Smoke from the blazing oil tanks and the exploding ammunition dumps covered the beaches. The wave of landing craft and LVTs found no difficulty passing through the gaps blasted in the offshore obstacles. Initial waves of troops on Red and Green beaches were able to go all the way to shore and land dry shod at 08:16 hours or one minutes after H-hour. The LVTs could not get ashore because of a sea wall about eight feet high. There was no enemy opposition but troops found a long ditch twenty feet wide and five feet deep that constituted an effective tank trap. Concrete pill boxes and other fortifications were not occupied.

The Engineer LCMs in waves five and six on both beaches could not reach shore and began to experience difficulties as they attempted to off load tanks and doziers in the deep soft mud. Only one tank was immobilized but most of the other vehicles bogged down. A few reached shore where they encountered the sea wall which the doziers were unable to breach immediately. The mud here was worse than at Morotai. The engineer boatman had their hands full just retracting their landing craft from the muddy beaches. The Boat Commander landed at Green Beach instead of Red Beach as planned. He established a command post and set up radio communications for control of the LCMs. Later is was learned that the Australians had established headquarters on Red Beach and then the boat company moved its control point to that beach.

LSTs began moving to shore shortly after 09:00 hours in order to take advantage of the high tide. By 10:00 hours all of the seven LSTs equipped with pontoons were grounded well offshore. The pontoons were adequate to link them to the beach. Vehicles began moving off, but the extremely limited beach area, the sea wall and the tank trap quickly led to dangerous congestion. The condition was corrected when the dozers ripped out the steel reinforcing wall and filled the tank trap ditch. Meanwhile the falling tide made it impossible for LCMs to use the beach for discharge of cargo and only a few small quantities of supplies were landed on the damaged piers. Yellow and part of Green beach could not be used for off loading because of the eight foot high sea wall.

Expansion of the beachhead was delayed when infantrymen advancing inland began meeting increased resistance. It had been the intention of the Engineer Boat Commander to put ashore on D-day the maintenance platoon and the medical personnel, but the crowded beach and the inability of the LCMs to land the platoon's bulldozer made the move impossible. Boat maintenance on D-day was carried out offshore where three LCMs underwent repair. The Engineers spent the night on their boats. On D-day plus one, in the afternoon, the LCMs began putting supplies on the piers by hand. By the second day the expansion of the beachhead gave the Engineers space ashore for their operations.

After D-day plus one, the operations of "B" company were concerned largely with the lighterage of cargo to the beach from offshore shipping. Landings on the beaches became progressively worse as the tidal range dropped from day to day. Boat maintenance personnel constructed an adequate beaching area for LCMs in order to keep an average of thirty five to forty craft working during the later phases of the operation. Boat control throughout the operation was excellent with the Engineer net working fine.

Shore installations of "B" company were under sniper fire and artillery fire at intervals during the early phases of the operation. Work was not interrupted and there were no casualties until 5 May when the Engineer officer was killed by a sniper. "B" company remained attached to the Australians until 31 May and they were engaged primarily in lighterage at Lingkas beach and on patrol missions. The company departed Tarakan on 31 May by their own landing craft to join "C" company and participate in the Brunei Bay operation. Six LCMs and their crews remained at Tarakan in support of the Australians. They remained there until September when the detachment joined the remainder of the company for transport to Batangas, Luzon in the Philippines.

This piece of equipment lifted up LCMs to do propeller work. Photo courtesy of Chester David.

Japanese war painting in custody of the U.S. Army of Occupation in Japan. Title: "Borneo Campaign," artist Kanabata Minoru. Collected at: Navy Museum. Period and remarks: 1942. Catalogue #35. Date: 18 November 1947. U.S. Army Signal Corps. Photo courtesy of the National Archives SC-301072.

LSTs high and dry on beach on Tarakan Island, Borneo D-Day, 1 May 1945, as seen from the USS Rocky Mount (AGS-3). Photo by cameramen on the Rocky Mount. Photo National Archives 80-G-49162.

An Australian Sargeant Remembers The Battle For Tarakan

After basic training I was appointed to a signals unit attached to the 17th Field Regiment (artillery) in Townsville. I was then sent for a short, but intensive wireless college course in Sydney. After training, the artillery regiment was being disbanded and I was sent to New Guinea to join the 26th Infantry Brigade of the Australian Ninth Division. At the amphibious landing at Lae, the 9th Division pushed the Japanese northward along the marsh and jungle littoral where more than half of the infantry battalion personnel succumbed to malaria, dysentery, tropical ulcers and scrub typhus. The crucial battle fought out in the Finisterre range at Sattleberg brought the highest military award, the Victoria Cross, to Sargeant "Diver" Derrick of the 2nd 48th/Battalion. He was later killed on Tarakan. I was hospitalized for two months in 1943 at the camp hospital at Koitaki with malaria, dysentery and tropical ulcers.

In April 1945, after jungle warfare and amphibious landing training on the Atherton Tableland and at Cairns, we embarked on the old Dutch ship, The Van Heuz, for Morotai Island, where we did more rehearsals for the Tarakan landing. Only one brigade of the 9th Division, the 26th Brigade was assigned the task of capturing Tarakan, while the other two brigades were held back to capture the Labuan Peninsula, later. As you know there was a foul up in intelligence as Tarakan proved by far the harder nut to crack. Of course we were well supported by US and Australian naval vessels, and American and Australian air forces. There was also a detachment of Netherlands East Indies troops under Dutch command.

We embarked at Morotai on the Manoora, an Australian coastal vessel, for Tarakan. I still have vivid recollections of the morning of May 1, 1945. Waiting in the belly of the ship for hours in full battle kit, laden to the hilt with heavy packs of personal equipment, rifle and ammunition, to say nothing of a heavy wireless set, the transistor had not yet been invented. Then stumbling our way through unlighted companionways to the upper deck where dawn had not yet broken but the oil fires on the beach struck fire in the skies and in our bellies. The order to scramble down the nets

to the assault boat below came as a relief from the tense hours of gut wrenching anticipation. A short wait as the ghostly form of a cruiser swept by to guide the first boats to the cleared channel to Red Beach, then the revving of engines sounded above a tremendous barrage of naval guns awoke the night sky, while shells exploded on the now visible beach. I remember my mate saying, "I only hope those bastards know when to hold their fire". I'm no hero, but I was too busy to sense fear. On landing I had to keep at the side of Major Owen Geddes awaiting his call for a connection to Brigadier Whitehead, the Commanding Officer of the operation, or to change quickly to another frequency as he spoke to one of the several infantry commanders. In hindsight I like to think I was chosen for that responsible job. Owen Geddes had often asked for me in previous operations, and in action we were a team in that we understood each other.

This LCM is shown alongside of a convoy supply ship loading supplies for the troops on the beach at Tarakan Island.

There were times when he asked for a conference of five COs when I could only contact four of them. He would nod, "I will go with four Sarge, but keep at five, I must get them in the next ten minutes." There was never any sign of concern or impatience.

I recall too, although in reflection, the feeling that I (we of course) were making history, If you will forgive my modesty and humility, as sure as generals and heroes of the school history book. After all this was only the third amphibious landing involving Australian troops in history and I had taken part in two of them. I was also aware that I was among the first troops of any of the Allied forces to invade Dutch territory. Add to this the fact that we were just a small force, one brigade with attached units, making the initial attack on the great island of legend history and adventure, Borneo.

But how this heroic image has been eroded down the following five decades! How cynical and disillusioned I have since become! How different the age faded reality from the exuberant romance of youth. Yet surely the heroic image is true, the cynicism false. What has changed is the public perception of our part in that campaign. Public sensitivity has been dulled and drugged by too much war. Too much sensation. Too much history. Too many heroes. Our children and grandchildren have never heard of the 9th Division, far less the 26th Brigade. Or of Borneo, far less Tarakan. My own disillusionment began perhaps on the night of May 1, 1945. We were pinned down on Red Beach which was under relentless enemy shell fire throughout the night. Although our infantry battalions had penetrated beyond the village of Lingkas, the town of Tarakan was being fiercely contested by desperate and courageous Japanese forces. Other troops had made some progress towards the prized goal, the airstrip, but days of hard fighting postponed its capture well beyond the scheduled date. In short, there were far more Japanese troops surprisingly well armed than we bargained for. But this campaign had been carefully planned for months. Yet the intelligence was obviously false, inadequate and incredibly inaccurate in so many ways.

My disenchantment grew. About the third night our Brigade Education Officer asked me if I could receive Radio Australia as he, a journalist by profession, would take the Australian news in shorthand for the big brass. I thought we would be headline news. I forget the detail but recall mainly my emotions at the time. There was only brief mention of Tarakan. Australians nor indeed Americans were not mentioned. An Allied force had landed at Tarakan Island off the coast of Borneo. Small pockets of resistance were being overcome and casualties were light. So much for my heroic vision. So much for my place in history. What audacious vanity to have experienced on D-day the greatest naval, artillery and air force barrage I had ever imagined or even want to witness again, then to believe it might have been mentioned on the national news.

The following night along Anzac Avenue, another operator and myself were on wireless duty in a slit trench though I think at the time I may have dozed off, as my mate was on watch. We were next to a group of perhaps two dozen Field Ambulance personnel. Apparently a Japanese soldier crept through the perimeter, armed with a 75 millimeter shell equipped with a three second fuse for use as a grenade and threw it into the field ambulance centre. Another version is that a drop short shell fired from one of our own ack-ack batteries, foolishly ordered from higher up the command to double as artillery, were firing at almost horizontal level. I was dazed and perhaps badly concussed. I have been deaf, very deaf, to this day. Far worse than the physical disability was the psychological trauma I have endured over fifty years in my work. I could never operate as a proficient wireless operator from that time. There is no record of my involvement in that incident, you see it was unthinkable at the time that I, as an NCO, would leave my post to report to some field medical centre that I was injured. The scene as dawn emerged is one that is so deeply burned into my psyche that I find it hard to write about. Enough to hint at scenes of death, moving mutilated bodies and body parts. The curl of a dead acquaintance protruding from the improvised ground sheet shroud. My illusions, too, died that night.

Slowly, too, I became skeptical of our very reason for being there. It became more obvious as the Tarakan, then the Labuan and Balikpapan campaigns progressed that MacArthur's grand plan did not really include Australian forces; that the Borneo campaign was strategically unimportant and it would not have any real effect on the outcome of the war with Japan.

After surrender and in deference to my hearing problem, I was given a job as an education officer, to help soldiers prepare for return to work after discharge. I spent time in a large white building that had survived the demolition of Tarakan town. I think it had been a residence of a high Dutch official before the war, and there were several Dutch officials staying there. They were there obviously to assert control over the native people, and to get the oil wells back to top production as soon as possible. I recall a pathetic attempt to gather native children to a sort of a picnic to celebrate Queen Wilhelmina's birthday. I became aware that at least a couple of these men held managerial positions in the pre-war oil company which I think was the Shell Company. Rightly or wrongly the horrible thought dawned on me that our whole campaign, the many lives that were lost, the lengthy list of sick and wounded and the whole costly project involving over eighty thousand men, planes, ships, tanks and munitions was basically to rehabilitate the Dutch colonies; worse still to restart the capital flow to oil magnates in Holland. Perhaps with the naivete and inexperience of youth I misjudged the situation, but nothing I have heard or read in the long years since has done anything to change my opinion.

All of this does not inhibit memories and nostalgia of comradeship or of shared experiences happy and dreadful. The quaint names that high features attract from leaders poring over maps that flowed through my earphones even now evoke emotional responses; Remember Margie, Snags Track, Freda, Milko, Butch, Spear, Peter, Sadie, Sykes, Helen, Otway and Jones.

Most of the trips I made on landing craft were short official missions. In addition to the landing on D-day I made another "amphibious" landing. A mate and I were with the 2nd 23rd Battalion during their attack on the Pamoesian village along John's Track. I passed on a message to the commanding officer that a sizable Japanese force had occupied Amal Beach at the end of the track, which had been previously cleared perhaps by air or naval bombing. As a result we had to accompany a platoon of "B" company back to Lingkas, on board an LCM, to make a landing while engaging the Nips on Amal Beach. When we got there the tide was high, too high to beach the LCM. Most of the platoon managed to swim ashore, or to keep their noses occasionally

above water, and, with their rifles and ammo held high above their heads, while they waded ashore. However, the Bren gunners and I were carrying far more poundage, he with the gun, I with a heavy wireless and battery in addition to my other swag. I saw him go down and, although he took a long time to emerge, his mates managed to help him ashore. Not so with me. I stayed down for what seemed an hour. I had trouble discarding the heavy gear below the surface. Then one of the U.S. soldiers must have found a long pole used for depthing and I eventually climbed up to be helped from the water. Whoever he was I guess I should thank him for rescuing me. All of this with a woodpecker and several snipers trying to pick us off. They got the Bren gun working in time, but they had no wireless communication for that night and most of the next day. I had a couple of other landing barge trips after the Japanese surrender at various points around the circumference of the island to mop up Japanese groups as they dispersed into individual groups to escape. The trouble was that many of them had not heard the war was over and they resisted. Few still had weapons, but some had strapped grenades to their bodies with the intention of suiciding on arrest. Most others came forward meekly. Later still I made a couple of longer trips as wireless operator for the Brigade Major and Intelligence Officer calling in at villages along the adjacent mainland coast, to announce that the war was over. Most villagers were glad to see us and we had cans of baked beans or bully beef to give out.

These are some of the remembrances of Sargeant Frank S. Snars of the Australian Army about his duties and observations while serving on Tarakan Island, Borneo from May 1945 to May 1946.

記　　　木舖　　　安

TJIENG SOEN ON
MEUBELMAKER
LADANG No. 43
TARAKAN BORNEO

Australians and U.S. troops watch a huge oil tank on Tarakan Island, Borneo, go up in smoke following naval shelling as they move inland. The walkie-talkie operator finds the heat too much and unslings his burden. Photo by H.A. Lederhandler, Pho M 1/c, U.S. Army Signal Corps. Photo: National Archives 80-G-49164.

The World War II Experiences of Thomas Ford, 2nd Field Company, Royal Australian Engineers, AIF, on Tarakan Island, Borneo.

On the first day of May 1945, at first light the invasion fleet moved into Tarakan and for an hour and a half Cruisers and Destroyers bombarded the beach areas. Rocket firing Gunboats ran close inshore to cover the assault craft, while four flights of heavy bombers dropped their bombs along the foreshore to reduce Japanese opposition to the beach landings.

On the LCI (Landing Craft Infantry) we had our company of two hundred fifty men waiting to land on the beach to carry out the jobs allotted to us. While waiting to go in a few of us were able to get up on deck to watch the bombardment of the beaches.

The noise was deafening, the destruction was horrific, nobody could have lived on the beaches. The Japanese had withdrawn back to the jungle, and had posted snipers in the trees to hold us up. The suspense of waiting to go ashore kept us in a state of uncertainty I was told later that it was the biggest bombardment anywhere in the Pacific up until this time.

Soon after the beach had had been taken, the six LCTs (Landing Craft Transport) and our LCI (Landing Craft Infantry) ran up on the beach approximately one and one half hours after the assault troops landed. Now it was our turn to do something towards the war effort.

After landing we were held up on the beach by Japanese snipers. We took advantage of the shelter under a high cliff until the assault troops could clear the snipers from the edge of the jungle. Throughout the morning the destroyers using five inch guns were called on to silence the snipers. The snipers had tied themselves on to the trees so, even though they may be wounded, they would not fall out of the tree, and could keep on firing. At times there would be no sniper fire for, maybe, half an hour. At one of those breaks, a mate of mine and myself decided to climb up a concrete stairway to see what was going on, first of all it was just our heads above the cliff, then it was head and shoulders. We couldn't see anything and all was quiet, so we thought they had got them. The next thing we knew bullets were flying all around us. We just about fell down the steps, and thanked our luck that he had missed:

Before our company had landed, we had been briefed on what type of jobs we would be doing, and who would be doing them. Of course this would depend on how the assault troops went. My job along with seven others was to make a runway for a light Auster spotting plane to take off and land. We were unable to move off the beach until mid afternoon, due to the Japanese snipers. But as the runway had to be completed, we left the shelter of the cliff and inspected the area. The plan was to make use of a portion of a sealed road, which was running down towards the beach. Between the end of the road and the beach there was a large unstable area that we had to cover with a steel mat especially made for surfacing airstrips. While we were inspecting the area, we had another burst of gun fire, well above our heads, aimed at a group of our sappers who were repairing the main jetty. Results were one sapper wounded.

We laid all the steel matting that had been unloaded for us, but it was not enough to cover the unstable area. Our Non Commissioned Officer called for more steel matting but there was no more available at that time. By this time we were into day two, and no more material to finish the job. The Royal Australian Air Force had already assembled the Auster aircraft and we were waiting on more matting. After some time we were called to other jobs, but we were to return when more matting arrived.

Sometime after we left, the pilot then decided that he would be able to take off on the two hundred yards of finished runway. The pilot and observer climbed aboard and proceeded to take off. I didn't see the actual takeoff but I did check on the accident later. I believe that once the plane ran off the matting and into the unstable area he couldn't make enough height and his wheels hit the large log lying across the end of the runway. The result was that the plane slewed, crashed and caught fire. The pilot was thrown from the plane but the observer was caught in the burning plane and died later of burns.

At one stage when we were waiting for more matting to arrive, three of us decided to look over a long building that was smoldering at one end but there were no flames so we entered through a door about half way down the building. There was nothing in the building but a few pieces of old

Native woman and child amid Aussies and Americans on the beach at Tarakan Island, near Bomeo, D-Day, 1st of May 1945. Photo by the USS Rocky Mount. Photo Nat. Archives 80-G-49159.

furniture, and no booby traps, not that you can always see them. We walked through the building to the top door and we were just about to walk out, when the other end of the building blew up. We left the building in a hurry, another lesson learned.

During the second day after the landing I was detailed to look after the main water pumping station, that pumped water up to the reservoir. I believe the pumping station was originally built by the Dutch before the war. During the war, either the Dutch or the Japanese had made the building bombproof by piling earth around the outside walls, leaving a bombproof screen at the entrance of the building. There were three large diesel engines and pumps in the building, but the Japanese had purposely damaged them beyond repair. The invasion planners must have realized that the engines would be damaged and had loaded two engines, pumps and equipment to cover a situation such as this. It was about 3:00 pm by the time I arrived at the pumping station, the engines and pumps had been assembled, the pipes and hoses connected up and everything was ready to start up.

The pumping station had to supply water to the reservoir for approximately thirteen thousand troops which consisted of Army, Navy, Air Force and U.S. personnel, plus two thousand Javanese civilians. It was essential that filtered water was available from the town supply because of the brackish water from the creeks and the risk of water borne disease. Outside of the building the water was drawn from either one or two small concrete dams that the creek water flowed through. After checking with the reservoir engineers, we started the engines and started pumping. After an hour or so of checking to make sure that the water was getting up to the reservoir, then it was left to me to take charge of the pumping station.

After awhile, I began to realize that I was in a very vulnerable position. The Japanese could easily infiltrate through to the building, even though they had been driven back into the jungles to their own prepared defenses. I was on my own and the jungle was only about four meters away on two sides, and I was to be there from daylight to dark, about fourteen to sixteen hours. I decided to make a small fort inside the open part of the building area, so that it covered the two side entrances and gave me some protection. All that I had was my rifle and fifty rounds of ammunition and two hand grenades. I don't think I would have lasted very long if the Japanese had thrown hand grenades or some sort of a bomb over the wall.

Every two hours or so I had to check the engines and pumps and walk out to the jungle side of the building to make sure the pump suction hoses were not blocked with creek rubbish. It was a very worrying time. I was there for three days and two nights, with one of those nights on guard duty, with nine other sappers, which meant that I was there for twenty four hours straight. The night that I was on guard, we made makeshift platforms to stand on so we could see over the wall. While I was on the platform, being very quiet, and listening with ears that stuck out like radars, I hear a thump, and almost straight away the mate just along from me called out, "I've dropped a hand grenade." Well, there is not much you can do when you are up on a platform and at least three seconds of a seven second fuse has gone. I just froze and hoped the pin was still in the hand grenade, luckily it was. That was another scare added to my collection.

During the late afternoon on my third day it was decided to man the pumping station with thirty men from one of the infantry battalions because the Japanese had been infiltrating the town area. As soon as the infantry arrived they started building a walk around the platform on the wall and made moveable barriers across the two entrances. About the time I left around 6:00 pm the area looked like an old time fort, with two men on each wall, and the remainder on standby. It proved to be the right move, especially for the sappers, because the Japanese attacked that night and the next morning there were two dead Japanese outside and none of our men were killed or wounded.

During my days at the pumping station, the company had moved into a large tin covered stores shed, which was just up from the beach area, it also had a loading platform across from the building. At the time that some of our stores had been unloaded, they stacked boxes of gelignite against the sides of the building about six feet high, and our small oil and fuel dump was located just around the corner of the building against the wall. On that day we had a Japanese plane come over, whether it was on reconnaissance, or if it intended to drop bombs I don't know, there was some light anti-aircraft fire and that may have frightened him off. We had all ducked for shelter behind whatever was available, and when it was over, we saw that the oil and fuel dump was on fire. How it started we didn't know, it could have been a bomb, the only thing we could think of was sabotage.

Before the air raid scare, I had been working on a truck that had hard starting, about fifteen feet out from the dump. There were no fire extinguishers handy, except at the beach area about a hundred yards away. One chap brought one up, but it was empty, another was brought up and it was empty as well. There were three large wheeled fire extinguishers unloaded, all empty. By this time the fire was out of control and the only thing we could do was to push the back out of the way. Two sappers were on each side of the truck, three were pushing on the front, I was walking along the right hand side with the door open steering the truck. We had just started to move when a petrol drum blew up. It sprayed the truck and the three sappers with flaming petrol, I was behind the open door so I had some protection. The clothing of the three in front was alight and two of them were rolled on the ground to put the burning clothing out. The other one ran off in panic, and as he ran past the raised loading platform an American Sea Bee (Beach Engineer) did a flying tackle and rolled him on the ground and put the burning clothing out. The three sappers were taken to the hospital, one very badly burned. The truck was a complete write-off.

While that drama was going on, another one was just starting. Earlier I had mentioned the explosives were stacked just around the corner from the fuel dump. While we were dealing with the first fire, fuel drums were still exploding, and the stack of gelignite in wooden boxes had caught alight. The truck was left to burn itself out, so we could attend the more serious fire. By this time the Commanding Officer and more men had arrived. He organized a continuous line and we handed the boxes on to the next in line to a safe distance away. Normally a plug of gelignite needed a detonator to explode it. But who knows what happens when the whole box is alight, and what happens when a stack is alight.

Everything went all right for a while but more boxes were catching alight, and boxes were already alight, were almost covered in flames. It was decided to abandon the line and take it in turn to run up, grab a box and run back. This way it only put three or four sappers at risk. The Commanding Officer was standing with boxes all around him, handing them to us as we came up. Either he knew more than us, that they wouldn't blow up or, he was a brave soldier. He had already been mentioned in dispatches in the Middle East. We finally moved the gelignite, some in very bad condition, to another location. The explosives were saved but the truck was completely burned out and of course we lost all our oil and fuel but we were able to replace the fuel.

Although the infantry had been fighting for three weeks our third camp was still only two kilometers from the beachhead. This camp was established beside the former Japanese Officers swimming pool and only a short distance from a building which had been destroyed but was obviously the Japanese occupation forces bank or mint. We didn't know whether they made money or just banked it. Myself and another engineer had heard about a tunnel located in the hill behind the bank or mint, the rumor was there was money hidden in the tunnel. Dutch money or Japanese invasion money. We didn't know but it seemed to be worth the risk of looking for it.

We found out that in the first three or four days of our landing, advancing infantry had blown both ends of the tunnel in to trap the Japanese who refused to come out. We had already been warned about , and had encountered booby traps, so there was a good chance that if Japanese soldiers had been trapped inside then booby traps could have been set. As we didn't want any of our officers or non-commissioned officers to know what we were about to do, and we didn't want it to become general knowledge, we quietly and selectively asked a few more mates to help. We had decided we needed a team of six to break into the tunnel and that we should tackle it from the far end which was out of sight of the camp. The pressures of war meant that we didn't have much time so at the first opportunity we started to clear away the rubble. Taking it in turn and using hand tools only, it didn't take the six of us long to make a small opening. Enlarging the hole further, we were able to make it big enough for one person at a time to look into the tunnel. The light from my torch penetrated the darkness in a very thin beam of light and did not light up the whole tunnel entrance. It proved to be the main entrance and the room was very large about ten meters by eight meters with a ceiling height of three meters. The room was surprisingly empty, the only thing obvious was a wooden lattice gate located on the left hand side of the far wall. On the other side of the gate there was a smaller tunnel about three meters by three meters.

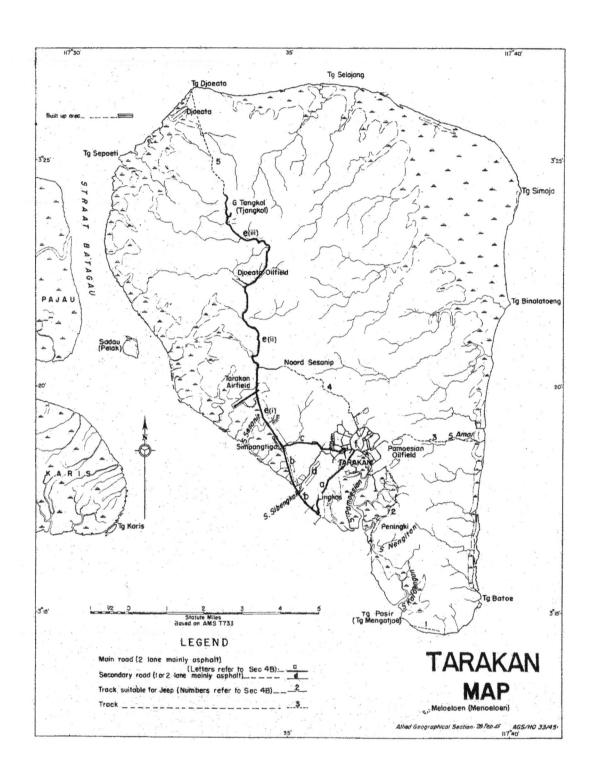

Built up area

Tg Djoeata

Tg Selajang

Djoeata

Tg Sepoeti

3°25'

STRAAT BATAGAU

G Tangkol (Tjangkol)

e(iii)

Djoeata Oilfield

PAJAU

Sadau (Pelak)

e(ii)

Noord Sesanip

Tg Simoja

3°25'

Tg Binalatoeng

20'

Tarakan Airfield

4

20'

e(i)

Simpangtiga

KARIS

S. Sesanip

c

b

d

a

f

TARAKAN

Pamoesian Oilfield

3 S. Amal

S. Pamoesian

Tg Karis

S. Sibengkok

b

ingkas

2

Peningki

S. Nengitan

3°15'

Tg Batoe

S. Karoengan

Tg Pasir (Tg Mengatjoe)

1

3°15'

Statute Miles
Based on AMS T733

LEGEND

Main road (2 lane mainly asphalt)
                    (Letters refer to Sec 4B) ___ a

Secondary road (1 or 2 lane mainly asphalt)___ d

Track suitable for Jeep (Numbers refer to Sec 4B)___ 2

Track _____ 3

TARAKAN
MAP

Meloeloen (Menoeloen)

Allied Geographical Section 28 Feb 45   AGS/HQ 33/45
117°40'

35'

At this stage none of us had entered the tunnel, all very wary of the possible existence of booby traps and the foul stale air within the tunnel. We lit quite a few matches just inside the entrance but they continually went out, so we knew there was not any oxygen to breathe. We needed to get air into the tunnel and we decided the best alternative was to make a small opening at the other end of the tunnel to create some flow from one end to the other. All without being seen. Anyway it did not do much good, especially in the time we had available. We had decided to go into the tunnel in pairs. We would hold our breath for as long as possible, look around and then would come out and let the next pair know what had been found and what was ahead. This would save time and valuable oxygen. The first pair entered the tunnel and within two minutes had returned. The entrance did not contain anything of any importance and luckily no booby traps. Then it was our turn to take a deep breath and dash in to see what we could find. We only managed to get as far as the gate but were able to force it open. The next pair didn't get far past the gate but they did find that the tunnel had another branch off to the right. As each of us returned to the opening from our search our half naked and tan bodies were unusually pale and the perspiration was pouring off of us. All of this in less than two minutes. It was getting close to 2400 hours so we decided to stop. We could not afford to be missed at the compulsory Mess Parade. We agreed if it was at all possible we should bring an air compressor back with us. By dubious means we managed to obtain a jeep and an air compressor and get back to the tunnel without suspicion. Air hoses connected to the compressor would allow us to venture deeper into the tunnel and still have air to breathe.

This time it was myself and my mate to go first and we would like to take the main left hand tunnel. I led into the tunnel, through the gate and up the left hand passage. The air lines meant that we did not rush as before, but unfortunately it was still difficult to see, as the torches showed only a very narrow beam of light. We cautiously walked further into the tunnel and had progressed about thirty feet when I stumbled forward onto what appeared at first to be a bundle of clothing. But with a closer look I realized as I had stumbled forward that I had put one foot through the chest and stomach of a Japanese soldier. Just imagine the horror and the smell from

the body which had probably been dead for two or three weeks. I can still remember that vividly until this day. After getting over the shock we found three Japanese laying-side by side across the floor of the tunnel. We didn't know how they died but presumed they committed Hari-Kari. Beside each one of them was their rifle and a small bundle of personal belongings. One of the bundles was wrapped in a Japanese flag. After checking it out as much as possible in the darkness we decided to return to the opening and inform the others. I took a rifle, bayonet and about a hundred rounds of ammunition. The other chap took one of the small bundles. The next pair went in past the bodies deeper into the tunnel but didn't find any thing of value, and certainly not the money that we thought was there. On the way out they picked up one of the small bundles.

It was about this time I was called back to camp for other more important duties. From there on I was not able to get back to the tunnel. The other chaps carried on looking through the right hand side of the tunnel but found no money or any thing of value, just piles of clothing. Perhaps it had just been a clothing and blanket store after all. The next day when our officers heard we had opened the tunnel the other chaps were ordered to close it.

Sabu (Dastigar), the East Indian actor who starred in "Elephant Boy" (1937) and "The Jungle Book" (1942), and other films, also served in the U.S. Army Air Corps in World War II as a nose-turret gunner on a B-24 Liberator, 307th Bombardment Group (HV), the "Long Rangers" of the 13th Army Air Force. (See page 34 for biography)

51

T/4 Chester P. David, Company "B", 593rd Engineer Boat & Shore Regiment, Boat Maintenance Section Remembers The Battle For Tarakan Island, Borneo.

When company "B" was ready to participate in the invasion of Tarakan Island in Borneo, we regrouped our company and spent a lot of time in Morotai Bay loading on a new type of assault craft called the Landing Ship Dock (LSD). This ship took on water and was partially submerged so we could run our landing craft (LCMs) inside it's well deck. The LSD then closed off the well deck docking area and pumped the water out leaving the landing craft sitting on the well area deck. When the LSD arrived at the invasion site the well deck was again flooded, the dock area gate opened and the LCMs floated out of the dock area.

The greatest thing I remember about the invasion of Tarakan was a lot of noise and confusion. Bombs were being dropped on the beach, Navy guns were firing on targets on shore and all the landing craft were churning at top speed for the beach. The water looked like it was boiling. Every place you turned there was a boat in front of you or alongside of you. Coming into the beach was great because we didn't have any trouble with the enemy. When morning came we had never seen such a sight! We hit the beach at high tide and when the tide went

out the LSD was left sitting on the bottom and you could see her propellers. We could barely get to the dock where we had tied the landing craft because the tide was so very low.

I had never seen so many bicycles in my life, they were the transportation of the island. We had fun riding them but had to return them because we got orders that they belonged to the people of the island and they would be very angry if we didn't return them.

Company "B" setup our company area on the beach where we could tie to the dock and from there we were taking infantry up the river and to places where they could find the enemy. In addition, we hauled clothing, canned food and other supplies from the Liberty in the harbor to the troops on shore. Every day there was some repair to be done on the boats because the salt water seemed to create many problems with the steel hulls of our landing craft. We patched and repaired the hulls and replaced the canvas gasket that sealed the ramp. To facilitate sanitary conditions we build an outhouse at the end of the pier complete with a toilet seat.

T/5 Ben R. Quigg, Company B, 593rd Engineer Boat & Shore Regiment Remembers The Fight For Tarakan Island, Borneo.

All of our "B" company landing craft were loaded on an LSD, Landing Ship Dock, to make the trip from Morotai Island to the assault landing at Tarakan Island. We made the landing after the Navy and Air Corps had softened up the beaches and knocked out some of the gun emplacements. An Australian light tank was loaded on our LCM and it proved too much of a load for the landing craft and we ran aground well short of the beach. An Australian General on shore was screaming "cowardice" but he stopped when he found we couldn't move anywhere on the mud flats along the beach areas. We finally dropped our ramp and the tank drove off into four feet of water and proceeded to shore. The timing of this landing

was to happen at extreme high tide to allow the LSTs, Landing Ship Tanks, to make it over the long mud flats. This worked good for the first time, but the next extreme high tide a month later was not as high as expected, leaving the unloaded LSTs still settled firmly in place on the mud flats. They called for a Navy sea going tug to pull them off the beach. Our LCM was assigned to pull the wire rope from the tug to the stem of the LST. This didn't work because the cable was so heavy it bogged us down a few feet short of the LST. Don't remember how the job got done but the tug couldn't budge the LST anyway.

On the first day we tied up to the end of the pier and we saw people on the pier were hiding behind

Left to right: General Sir Thomas Blamey, the Commander-in-Chief of the Australian Military Forces; General Douglas MacArthur, Commander-in-Chief of the Southwest Pacific Area; and John Curtin, the Prime Minister of Australia (1941-1945). They are discussing the war in the Southwest Pacific. AWM042766. This photograph is a gift from Dr. Peter Stanley of Canberra, Australia and was first used in his book, "Tarakan, an Australian Tragedy." Photo courtesy of Thomas B. Ford.

Left to right: Brigadier David Whitehead and Lieutenant General Sir Leslie Morshead, Commander of the 1st Australian Corps. These two gentlemen are meeting at Brigadier Whitehead's headquarters on Tarakan Island, May 4, 1945. AWM090967. This photograph is a gift from Dr. Peter Stanley of Canberra, Australia and was first used in his book, "Tarakan, an Australian Tragedy." Photo courtesy of Thomas B. Ford.

A discussion of plans of operation on Tarakan Island off of Borneo. Left to right: Brigadier David Whitehead; Lieutenant General Frank Berryman and General Sir Thomas Blamey. AWM089771. This photograph is a gift from Dr. Peter Stanley of Canberra, Australia and was first used in his book, "Tarakan, An Australian Tragedy." Photo courtesy of Thomas B. Ford, formerly of the R.A.E., attached to the 9th Australian Division (commonly known as the "Rats of Tobruk").

three inch thick planks for protection from sniper fire occurring several hundred yards away on shore. Soon we realized those splashes a few feet from our stem were from a 25 caliber Japanese rifle. I made myself scarce because I felt they were getting personal about the matter of trying to kill us. I was sure glad their "Kentucky windage" was just a tad off. If they had corrected properly things might have turned out differently. The people on top of the pier felt a little sheepish about hiding behind the three inch planks. It sure made sense when caught in the open to find something to hide behind. Before long responding shots were fired and then all was quiet.

Several nights after the initial landing "Washing machine Charlie" flew over. There was beautiful fireworks with tracers and searchlights focused on him. He kept on flying and never returned. "Washing machine Charlie" was an affectionate name bestowed on Japanese nuisance flights that usually harassed the troops at night. The plane used most nights on these raids was a "Betty", twin engine Mitsubishi medium bomber.

The first week in June 1945 we departed Tarakan Island for Tawi Tawi Island where our boat and a picket boat remained behind for repairs. The remainder of the company proceeded to Palawan Island and we caught up with them the following day. The convoy proceeded to Brunei Bay, Borneo and Labuan Island to participate in the assault landing in that area on the morning of 10 June 1945.

Roy Williams, 2nd Field Coy Royal Australian Engineers A.I.F.

Some weeks before the landing on Tarakan, I was put into hospital in Morotai suffering badly with dermatitis, which meant that I missed out on the landing on Tarakan, finally arriving about 2 or 3 weeks later.

When I arrived, the Company was camped in the old Dutch Oil field workshop depot, which had a main road on one side and a swamp on the other side. For some weeks the Japanese had been infiltrating through the Base area, some of them carrying shells which were fused ready to explode when they were dropped on the ground. Others had bayonets tied to bamboo poles. Some Japanese were trying to get to the beach to get a boat to escape to Borneo. Around the workshop depot yard was a six-foot high chain fence, which made us feel a lot safer, because of the infiltrating Japanese. Although the main track to the Javanese Kampong (village) was on the other side of the swamp, the Javanese could walk past the camp side of the swamp to get to the main track. They were allowed to use the main track during the daytime, but had been warned about using it at night. I was on guard duty myself, when we heard footsteps, not knowing whether they were Japs or Javanese, we challenged them, lucky for them they were Javanese, but if we had been trigger happy, they could have been shot.

After the Japanese had been pushed back out of their main defensive pockets, and the main fighting had finished, we got the idea of finding a boat we could use for fishing, to supplement our boring diet of tinned stew. We eventually found a boat, which had been the Harbour Masters launch. It was pulled up on the beach and it was badly in need of repair. This was no great problem, as not only had I built and repaired boats, there were two boat builders in the unit. The boat was about 25-30 foot long, of a semi-planing type and could carry about 10 people. While we were repairing the woodwork, we also had to find an engine and gearbox. We were lucky to find a Ford V8 engine and gearbox in a damaged truck. The biggest problem was a suitable shaft and propeller, which we eventually found on a boat that had been sunk up one of the creeks. Three Sappers and myself were detailed to look after the boat, which meant that we were camped on the end of the pier. In the tropics and especially in this area the tide rose and fell about 10 feet, so allowance had to be made for this when mooring the boat. The boat was mainly used for fishing, but it had other uses, such as taking small groups on inspections of beaches etc. The fishing was done using gelignite, which stunned the fish, and as they floated to the surface we scooped them up. Fish caught this way, had to be eaten as soon as possible. There was a 5-foot long Grouper fish, which we thought would make a good meal for the Company, but it was hard to get at as it was under the pier. We lowered a hand grenade, which was jammed in a condensed milk can, down beside it, but we didn't get it, probably because the hand grenade was not very effective in water. We found a special place where we only fished occasionally, it had been a Catalina dock, which had been sunk before the Japanese captured the Island. It was in this spot that we caught a fish called Trevally, which were beautiful when cooked in butter.

Opposite on the other side of the pier, were about 10 American PT boats. They were wooden boats, and had 3 Allison aircraft engines, which gave them approximately 4500 HP. They could travel at about 50 knots and were very spectacular going at full speed with a great rooster's tail behind them. They used to cruise around the Island, and up the rivers in Borneo looking for Japanese. The Americans lived very well, and we were able to swap fresh fish for fresh bread and butter. We arranged with them for a trip on one of their boats, but missed out when the war ended.

Being stationed on the end of the pier, brought us in contact with many sights and different people, one type in question was the Dyaks from Borneo. They had been head hunters all their lives, and as they had been mistreated by the Japanese, it was no trouble to place a bounty of half a bag of rice for each head brought in by the Dyaks. The Dyaks also caught and brought Japanese prisoners in, to hand over to the authorities. I was on the pier when the Dyaks brought in a number of Japanese, and handed them over to the NICA (Netherlands Indies Civil Affairs) soldiers. The Japanese were that weak they could hardly stand up, but that didn't stop the NICA soldiers from badly mistreating them.

On one of our beach inspections, to the south of the Island, which was about 3 miles from where we landed on Day One. We noticed a beach area beside a small creek that had been used for some type of operation because it had a light railway line down the beach. Although the main fighting had finished on Tarakan, there were still pockets of Japanese hiding in the jungle and infiltrating into the Base area looking for food, so we had to be on the lookout. We landed on the beach, and although there were other signs of previous occupation, we followed the railway line which led into a fairly large tunnel, investigating further, we found a torpedo, which led us to believe that it may have been a small submarine base (refueling etc.). As two torpedoes were fired at the ships during the initial landing. Not from a submarine, but from the beach, this may have been the beach they were fired from. None of the ships were hit.

After the war had officially ended, we decided to take the boat over to Borneo and travel up the Sesajap River (incidentally Borneo was out of bounds to us). We motored/sailed across the Batagau Strait which was the sea lane between Tarakan and mainland Borneo, the distance was about one to two miles. Then we motored up the Sesajap River until we came to a native village. The natives were on the side of the bank calling out "Nippon, Nippon," we landed to see what it was all about, and found out that the Japs had been there two days ago.

We didn't go looking for Japanese who most likely didn't know the war had ended, so we got back on the boat, and finally back to Tarakan.

WAR GRAVES – TARAKAN

Poem by F/O T.O. Latham

Will you walk with me in the heat of day,
Till we come at the cross-roads on the way
Of a dusty road on Tarakan,
To a scene in the scheme of the war's mad plan.

There are soldiers there in a little square,
Who will breathe no more of the dust-filled air.
On the trails they died, by the road they rest,
With the foreign soil on each manly chest.

On the crosses which mark the arid mounds
Are the tales of courage which knew no bounds,
"Killed in Action" and "Died of Wounds"
But the wasted lives are the war's worst ruins.

You will see their mates at the gravesides stand
Quietly, slouch hats held in hand,
And you may grieve, as they will too,
For the hopes and dreams which will not come true.

In death these men have but simple needs,
No separate tracts for differing creeds,
For the shoulders which never were cold in life
Are together in death as they were in strife.

You may gaze at the flag which hangs from the mast
To honour the men who were staunch till the last,
And fancy you hear a quiet voice say
"Australia, my country, will you repay?"

"Will you warm my hearth, give daily bread
To the hungry mouths which once were fed
Through the sweat and toil of a fallen man,
Who sleeps by the road on Tarakan?"

So when you return, by the dusty road,
You may bear your share of a sacred load,
With a pride whose flame ignited then,
Will burn till the sound of the last Amen.

LCMs from Company "B" on their way to Brunei Bay from Tarakan Island. The hospital ship "HOPE" is in the background. This photo was taken off of North Borneo near the Island of Tawi Tawi in early June 1945. Photo by John McCreagh, a medic in Captain "Doc" Bean's Medical Detachment.

General Of The Army Douglas MacArthur

General MacArthur graduated from West Point Academy, New York in 1903 with the highest honors in his class. During World War I, he served in the 42nd Rainbow Division as Chief of Staff, in France. When he was selected as Chief of Staff of the Army in 1930, he was promoted to full General. In 1937 he retired and was recalled to active duty in July 1941 to take over the Philippine Command. After the declaration of war with Japan in December 1941, he directed a delaying action against the Japanese invaders until he was ordered to Australia to take command of the Allied Forces in the Southwest Pacific Theater of Operations. He was appointed Allied Commander of the Japanese Occupation Forces after the surrender of Japan. When the Korean Conflict broke out he was appointed to command the United Nations Forces in Korea.

CHAPTER 6
Brunei Bay

The second assault on the Japanese held positions in Borneo took place in the Brunei Bay area of the northwestern coast of the island. This operation was a simultaneous landing on all three beaches in the bay area. The three areas were Labuan Island, Muara Island and the mainland approach to the town of Brunei.

In accordance with orders issued by GHQ SWPA and Oboe VI operation would be carried out primarily by the First Australian Corps, reinforced by United States units and supported by Allied Naval and Air Forces. The Australian commander put together forces including the 20th and 24th Australian Infantry Brigade Groups of the 9th Australian Division. All troops were to be Australian except the 727th Amphibious Tractor Battalion, minus one company, the Boat Battalion of the 593rd Engineer Boat & Shore Regiment, minus one company, and the 1463rd Engineer Maintenance Company, less one detachment.

Planning for Oboe VI was done at Morotai Island at about the time "B" company was staging for the Oboe I assault on Tarakan Island. Thus "B" company could not be included in the planning. "A" and "C" companies were planned for the Brunei operation. However, before "A" company could be included, they were designated for the next Borneo landing to be at Balikpapan. Since two boat companies would be required at Brunei it was decided to add "B" company assuming the operation at Tarakan would permit the company to leave.

"C" company equipment and landing craft was transported from the staging area at Morotai Island to Brunei Bay as follows: LSD Carter Hall; 18 LCMs and 2 "J" Boats; by other means, towed or under their own power, 8 LCMs; 1 LCM Gunboat; 2 regimental crash boats; 2 maintenance LCMs. Other shipping; 9 LCMs; Liberty Ships; 5 LCMs and 1 LCM Gunboat. Supply Ships would tow an LCM Rocket Boat; 3 Picket Boats; and two fuel barges to Tarakan to join "B" company's convoy moving to Brunei.

On 31 May, "B" company joined the convoy from Morotai and the group proceeded to Brunei. Six of the "B" company LCMs remained at Tarakan with twelve crew members for the support of the Australian ground troops. The convoy was made up of 41 cargo LCMs, 2 LCM gunboats, 1 LCM maintenance boat, 3 picket boats, 2 fuel barges and the LCM rocket boat. The group, traveling under their own power, through the Tawi Tawi Islands in the Sulu archipelago reached Balabac Island on 6 June 1945. The main assault group convoy departed Morotai on 4 June 1945 and it consisted of 85 transports and other ships. As the convoy neared the coast of Borneo it was joined by the USS Boise with General MacArthur aboard.

Ships and landing craft participating in the D-day operation arrived at Brunei Bay at 07:00 hours 10 June 1945 and anchored off Victoria Harbor, Labuan Island. Landing craft were launched immediately. Only one Japanese plane dropped a bomb near an APA but it missed the target, H-hour on the beaches was 09:15 hours. At 08:05 hours naval bombardment of all beaches began and at 08:20 hours the air strikes began. The seas were calm and the sky was clear, an ideal situation for a successful landing.

At 12:00 hours on D-day plus one the "B" company convoy from Tarakan and the remainder of "C" company that had joined the convoy enroute arrived at Brunei Bay. The long trip by company craft was made without incident but a third of the boats needed maintenance. Some of the LCMs were placed in service immediately upon arrival. After this convoy arrived the Boat Battalion had more than 70 LCMs at Brunei Bay as well as gunboats, rocket boats, fuel boat, maintenance craft and "J" boats.

Landing plans showed the attacking forces to land on three different beaches at the same time. The locations were Brunei Bay, Brown Beach on Labuan Island at the mouth of the bay; Green Beach in an area called Brunei Bluff and on White Beach on the east end of Muara Island. Two other beaches were also marked, Yellow Beach near Green Beach, Red Beach near White Beach and these were to be taken by troops moving overland after the initial landings.

Troops were put ashore on Brown and White Beaches in LVTs of the Amphibious Tractor Battalion and at Green Beach by the Navy LCVPs. The Boat Battalion was to use their LCMs to land tanks and heavy equipment ashore. Engineer landing craft available for D-day landings were those of "C" company since "B" company had to travel from Tarakan by it's own landing craft on the 700 mile trip to Brunei and were not available for the initial landings. Their landing craft had to be serviced before they could be put into service.

Admiral Forrest Beton Royal
Leader of the Naval Amphibious Units on Borneo
World War II 1945

He was commander of the Naval Amphibious Group in the beachhead landing assaults on Leyte, Luzon, Mindanao and Borneo In 1944 and 1945. Rear Admiral Royal was skilled in Amphibious Warfare, his brilliant planning and execution led to his many successful operations against the enemy. He was recognized for his important assignments with the award of the Distinguished Service Medal and the award of a Gold Star in lieu of a second Distinguished Service Medal. On 18 June 1945, he died aboard his flagship.

The invasion forces landed on D-day at Brown Beach near the town of Labuan. This location was chosen because it was the only area free of coral reefs. One Australian unit moved out to the east along the Coal Point Road with the primary objective being the capture of the Labuan Airfield. The other unit moved northeast and north to take the Government House, then proceeded along Hamilton Road, northwesterly and capture Timbalai Airfield.

After the Government House and the two airfields had been captured and most of the enemy had been killed or captured there remained a pocket of enemy troops that had been bypassed. The enemy pocket was approximately one half square mile of dense woods surrounded by mangrove swamps. This area had been under intense artillery fire since the 13 of June and by 17 June, Australian tank units had control of all approaches to the enemy pocket.

Late on the 20th of June two groups of the Japanese attempted to escape the pocket. One group of fifty or sixty of the enemy made their way out of the pocket and moved through the mangrove swamp to the Amphibious Engineer camp site, located just north of the town of Labuan. The Amphibs killed forty three of the Japanese on the morning of 21 June. That same day the Australians killed or captured the remainder of those Japanese in the pocket.

When the initial landings had been completed and the five beachheads secured, the Australian Forces pushed south and east on the mainland against the enemy. The towns of Brooketown, Brunei and Limbang were captured using the LCM gunboats and rocket boats. Since the road system was limited and inadequate LCMs, were used as "water taxis" to move troops and artillery up the rivers to surprise the enemy in their inland positions.

When the Brunei operation was secure, the 20th Infantry Brigade, 9th Australian Division moved its headquarters to Kuala Belait. Here the brigade commander had to make use of the river highway to thwart the activity of the enemy. A detachment of amphibious craft consisting of four LCMs and a gunboat began probing the inland rivers and coastal defenses by water borne patrol. The operational area for these patrols was extensive. The area covered was from Tutong to Miri coastwise and inland navigating the Mendarum, Belait and Baram rivers. All missions for the amphibious craft were for combat patrol or resupply.

On the 14th of July the most extensive river operation called on by boats of the amphibious battalion to perform was the patrol up the Baram river to Marudi. One gunboat and three LCMs with an infantry force of one company reinforced by supporting weapons, comprised the striking force at Marudi, a point sixty miles from the mouth of the Baram river. Leading the assault formation while underway was a cargo LCM as a point. This LCM had its cargo shipped with a center aisle clear. The supplies were stacked along the port and starboard quarters of the well deck at a height no greater than would afford infantry small arms and automatic weapons, some protective concealment from the well itself.

The Japanese, expecting the Aussies to travel overland to the town were caught by surprise when the artillery opened up on them and the Aussie patrols made a complete encirclement of their positions. A major victory was accomplished with only slight casualties and several months ahead of schedule. To bolster the swift advance, LCMs were loaded so heavily that their bows were lower than their sterns, as they rushed tanks, trucks and other heavy equipment to the forward areas.

The gunboat with its 20 millimeter guns was used tactically as a support element for this operation. The other two LCMs carried the reserve elements and enough supplies, ammunition, fuel for the craft and water for the nine day operation. A Catalina flying boat provided aerial reconnaissance and was in communication with the 20th Australian brigade at all times. Carrier pigeons were also used by the infantry elements for emergency communications. Evacuation of casualties was by LCM and for seriously wounded by Catalina flying boat.

Some of the rivers traveled by the 593rd boats in Borneo were barely navigable at some points and only wide enough for one small craft to pass through at a time. In several places, crew members had to stand on the ramps of the LCMs with machetes and cut away the over hanging limbs of trees and dense mangroves that form a virtual archway over the water.

On 20 June 1945, one LCM left Limbang to travel up river as far as possible, loaded with Australians and native Dyaks. The purpose of the

Officers headquarters on Labuan Island, Brunei Bay, Borneo, 1945. Photo courtesy of James C. Merrill.

Company "C" headquarters on Labuan Island, Borneo, 1945. Photo courtesy of James C. Merrill.

The DE (Destroyer Escort), the "Flagship" for the Invasion of Brunei Bay, Borneo. Photo courtesy of James C. Merrill, who was the radio operator and the liaison for the invasion of Brunei Bay and Labuan Island.

mission was to find Australian, British and United States prisoners of war that were reported being held at the headwaters of the Limbang river. The trip was entirely successful, operationally, but the mission was a failure as no prisoners were found. Some Australians were there, in command of three thousand Dyaks who had been organized to hunt down the Japanese. The LCM crew was entertained and fed by a Dyak family who announced they were the first white people to reach that point since 1941. Leaving a U.S. Counter Intelligence Corps officer and an Australian patrol, the LCM returned to Limbang. In the meantime the gunboat and the two LCMs made a mission up the Brunei river to evacuate two Australian platoons who had been chasing fleeing Japanese troops. On each of these several excursions, wounded, prisoners, liberated natives, Javanese and others were brought back to Brunei. On 23 June 1945, one LCM took off to reach the headwaters of the Pandaruan river in search for a body of Japanese reported in the area. A strong Australian patrol was carried. On the arrival of the mission in the area it was reported that all Japanese had evacuated the area. Several tributaries of the river were explored and the natives brought in some Japanese prisoners. The natives reported that the enemy troops had evacuated to the southwest, looting native gardens and carrying away with them their cattle and their food stores. At 15:00 hours that day, the Dyaks brought in freshly cut heads of a Japanese doctor, his wife and baby.

To say these river journeys passed without incident would be far from the truth. Brigade boatmen in Borneo have had many interesting adventures. At one time or another they have run into small parties of Japanese which were wiped out in short order when the twin .50 caliber machine guns of the LCMs were turned on them. One boat surprised twelve Jap soldiers swimming in the river apparently totally unaware of the swift advance of the Amphibian Engineers in the new "river warfare." They scurried out of the water without stopping to pick up their clothing.

One Amphib remarked as his boat threaded its way up one of the Borneo rivers, "The last time I saw this place was in a Frank Buck adventure movie." For that matter, most of the rivers in Borneo haven't had a white man on them in three to five years. Surprised and grateful natives often give the crew members chickens and eggs and other food stuffs in trade for what they consider a delicacy, canned corn beef.

LCMs in the vicinity of Brunei Town near the Miri and Seria oil fields often pass the famous Dyaks, a head hunting tribe of natives. It is not unusual for the boat crew to report seeing a Dyak warrior standing on the river bank holding the head of a Japanese in one hand and beating his chest with the other. Incidentally, these Dyaks have been very happy since the British have allowed them to practice their old custom of head hunting.

River warfare, at its best, is a maneuver requiring daring and fortitude. LCMs carefully pick their way up the river never quite knowing whether the enemy is ready to ambush them at the next bend of the river or if they are lurking in the thick jungle fringe on the banks. The Padas river in the Brunei Bay area of Borneo is a typical example of the type of river that has all the elements of what constitutes a dangerous over water route. It is a mass of curves and both banks are lined with dense mangrove and jungle growth.

LCMs of the boat battalion scouted the river within three miles of the Japanese held town of Beaufort, some thirty miles from the mouth of the Padas. When no opposition was encountered, a sizable force of Australian ground troops and a large number of artillery pieces were transported by the LCMs to a staging area for the ultimate capture of the town.

When the LCMs of the boat battalion probed the Klias river of Northern Borneo in search of Japanese strongholds they found instead a Chinese doctor and his English wife who had been dodging the Japanese for three and a half years. The Amphibs spotted the couple frantically waving on the banks of the upper reaches of the river. After being assured that they were not Japanese, the LCM pulled into shore, lowered the ramp and welcomed Dr. and Mrs. Liem Ping Thien, formerly of Jesselton, North Borneo. Before the war Dr. Liem had a thriving practice among the white population and he also worked for one of the large rubber companies. When the Japanese occupied the Jesselton area they interned Mrs. Liem for six months but later released her to work with her husband in caring for the civilians. The Japanese made life miserable for them so they took to the jungles and hid the best that they could. Two of their faithful Chinese servants helped make life somewhat bearable for them in the jungles.

The Amphibs brought them back to the main base where they provided much valuable information about the enemy. They now planned to remain in Borneo for several more years until they could replenish the funds that had been taken by the Japanese. The Doctor's contract with the rubber company was to have expired the 30th of December 1941 and he and his wife had planned to return to England at that time after eight years in Borneo. The Doctor helped the Allies by working in an Australian medical clearing station and his wife worked as a nurse in the front lines of the Borneo fighting.

The 593rd EB&SR Helps Shorten The War.

(The following is an excerpt from the 15 July 1945 issue of the *RAMP*)

With the Third Engineer Special Brigade on Borneo. Veteran Australian troops are giving much of the credit for their lightning reconquest of the oil center of Borneo to the Amphibian Engineers of the Boat Battalion of the 593rd Engineer Boat & Shore Regiment The Amphibs are virtually the only American troops, outside the Navy, to support what is almost entirely an Australian show. Those boat companies operating the LCMs of the 593rd have engaged in three major operations of landing the assault troops on the beaches of Tarakan, the Brunei Bay area and Balikpapan.

On the first operation on Tarakan Island, "B" company of the 593rd practically saved the day when its LCMs unloaded cargo from stranded LSTs lying offshore and brought the supplies right up to the soldiers on the beaches. Companies "B and "C" carried out simultaneous landings in the Brunei Bay area in what correspondents described as one of the most complicated operations of the Pacific War. At Balikpapan, company "A" repeated these complicated landing tactics.

Australian Army Officers have been high in their praise of these units of the Third Engineer Special Brigade. One Brigadier of the 9th Australian Division, a veteran of the Middle East and the New Guinea campaigns, told a Third ESB correspondent that the 593rd's river and beach work had sliced from two to three months from the Borneo fighting schedule. Also, an American technical and tactical observer with the Australian forces, Colonel R.H.

McKinnon, remarked to the correspondent, "Your boys are doing a hell of a fine job."

AN ARMY TUG CREW GETS SOME JAPS
(The following is an excerpt from the 24 June 1945, volume XI No. 18 of the *RAMP*).

"The Air Corps has nothing on us, we are going to paint a Jap flag and a raft on our boat," grinned the crew members of the ST 384, a tug boat manned by brigade personnel who recently destroyed a Jap raft and sent three Japs to a watery grave. The tugboat spotted the raft many miles at sea and moved to within fifty yards of it for a look see. It appeared empty but piles of leaves aroused suspicion. While they were debating what to do, an empty LCM that was being towed swung around on its tow line and smacked the raft. Three Japs piled out from under the leaves on the raft. Now honorable Jap radio may report three Nippon sons killed in South Pacific naval battle.

SPIRITUAL GUIDANCE
(This is an excerpt from the 24 June 1945, Volume XI, No. 18 issue of the *RAMP*).

For two of the Third Brigade Chaplains, and the Chaplain's Assistant, the show actually started when their LSD nosed out of the base of departure and headed for Brunei Bay. They represented the spiritual guidance for both Army and Navy personnel aboard the ship and they held services often during the voyage. The services were well attended.

The "C" company command post was located about a half mile from the beach in an abandoned building next door to a Chinese Temple and an undertaking enterprise. The temple had been an ordinary one story building at one time, but the Buddhist Priest for ten years had occupied the building and conducted his services in the front portion of the edifice and had an undertaking business in the back room. Several teak wood coffins were found measuring somewhere between six and a half and seven feet in length. The sides and top were of a rounded effect and they were stained solid black on the outside.

They had found the priest during the early stage of the landing immediately after the bombing. He had stayed in the temple all through the unmerciful naval pounding of the town and was found under a little table sitting next to the wall. The table had been covered with a mat and only his legs were showing. He was scared and suffering from shock. Later several Amphibs built up his morale with nothing more staple than fresh crispy, crunchy K-rations "dog" biscuits.

There was a little kitchen near the "C" company command post and a dead Chinese lay on the floor. The Chaplain suggested if there were any more around, they should all be buried. One more shattered corpse of another Chinese in a nearby dwelling and the two bodies were comfortably laid to rest.

An Amphib Recounts A Memorable Experience In The River Warfare in Borneo. The Day Was A Thousand Years
By: J. Ben Lit

In May 1940, during World War II, the Germans had cut off the British at the Port of Dunkirk, France. An evacuation of troops, avoiding surrender, successfully was accomplished by utilizing hundreds of small civilian pleasure craft.

The miraculous success of this venture, indicated the wartime need for amphibious units comprised of many small craft capable of landing at a beach, accepting or discharging cargo, i.e. troops, equipment, food, etc., and pulling back off the beach.

In early 1942, the US Army Engineers were directed to organize the Amphibian Engineers, Army Special Brigades. Their principle craft was to be the LCM, Landing Craft Mechanized, a fifty-foot Higgins boat, with the aforementioned capabilities.

The initial training was at Camp Edwards, on Cape Cod, Massachusetts. Six brigades were formed. They were sent to both European and the Southwest Pacific Theaters of war. Nearly every Division of Infantry, where needed, would have a company of amphibians as their "private" navy. This facilitated the movement of infantry, whether hedgehopping the shore line or using riverways, in pursuit of the enemy.

The story following is an actual event. At the time we were attached to an Australian Infantry company, and engaged primarily in river patrol duty.

The murky river parted as our Army Amphibian Craft, M9C9, chugged her way forward. Dense jungle growth along the banks responded to the lapping waves. An occasional crocodile, seemingly undisturbed, slithered into the water. The excited "cheet cheet" of monkeys heralded our entry into the wilds of Borneo. The day was born, past is make believe, almost as if it never was. So it is with all those weird adventures of yester years, lingering in the sub-conscious, true, yet not true, happening, yet almost if they hadn't happened.

The date, long ago, July 11, 1945, the place, obscurity, Limbang, Borneo, the mission, proceed to village eight up river, arrest one specific Malayan, proceed fifteen miles further up river to Dyak village, turn prisoner over to Australian commando for trial as a Japanese spy.

Johnny, with a tense look on his face, skillfully maneuvered the craft upstream. Moe, the engineer, smiled with self satisfaction as the twin diesels roared and thrust the craft deliberately forward. Myself, as seaman, anxiously stood watch, on a cat walk up forward. In the well deck, the Australian patrol relaxed in the security of the surrounding steel. They were enjoying the ride.

The Malayan village lay ahead. Johnny carefully beached the craft while Moe and I teamed to secure a line to a nearby tree. The Australians disembarked, their metal cleated combat boots clanking on the steel of the well deck. The suspected spy was quickly apprehended and almost willingly yielded to the request of the Australian officer to accompany us to the Dyak village.

Twin diesels roared again as M9C9 continued her journey upstream. Clouds were beginning to fill the sky as if to shield the heavens from the events about to unfold. Our captive, the unsuspecting "spy" sat quietly on the steel deck. His age, often difficult to guess on Orientals, was perhaps forty five. He was slight of build, fairly well dressed in neatly cared for khakis, and outwardly unconcerned with his plight. As noon time approached, we offered him "K" rations, our favorite disposable food. He munched thoughtfully on the jaw challenging biscuits. His eyes gazed unseemingly forward.

The face, can I ever forget that face. Timid, yes, timid, yet friendly, unsuspecting, yet frightened. Confidence shone forth from his eyes, yet apprehension was evident. His wan smile indicted innocence, yet the grimness of reality was apparent.

The lush jungle seemed to converge as the river narrowed. M9C9 slowed as though in hesitation of the approaching Dyak Village. The increasing current of the river seemed to strive to hold back time, to deter the horrendous acts of men about to unfold.

Johnny eased the boat alongside the small mooring. The prisoner paled as a roar from the Dyak tribesmen signaled the journeys end. Despite the tropical heat, a chill spread through my body. Few white men had ventured this far into the Borneo wilds, fewer had returned.

The Dyaks crowded the beach area. Many had never seen the steel monster LCM. Those that had, gestured with "I told you so" chatterings. Indeed, to some, the boat must have appeared as the "Merrimac" or "Monitor" did to early Americans.

We had observed these "wild men" before, but never in these numbers, or in this close proximity.

As the Aussies and their prisoner disembarked, a white man leading a pack of Dyaks approached to greet us. His appearance was striking in that he was dressed in an Australian uniform, except he was wearing short pants. His jaunty stride lacked but a riding crop in hand to remind one of a typified British officer so frequently depicted in the movies. The shock of blond hair and ruggedly handsome features reminded one of an "Alan Ladd" character. His age, early twenties. We approached and were introduced to this Australian commando. He told us of parachuting into this area "D" minus sixty days. His story unfolded telling of the immediate friendliness of these Dyaks mainly by mistreatment by the Japanese. He told us of how arms and supplies are dropped, how he organized the Dyaks into a fighting force and of how they harassed and decimated the retreating Japanese armies.

The cold glint of his steel blue eyes told the story of a soldier, indoctrinated-in hate, merciless in slaughter, and fearless in obedience. Indeed, he related that the only time he felt real fear was prior to his "jump." His captain had provided him with pills and ordered him to take same if the natives were unfriendly.

The trial began. The prisoner was brought forth to face the commando, judge, jury and god. Gibberish of an accusing, pointing Dyak told the story. The accused had worked for the Japanese as a collector of "taxes." Each Dyak was required to provide a specified quantity of rice to the Japanese. This Dyak told of being beaten by the Japanese because he had

failed to provide his quota. The Dyak, again pointing, blamed the accused for his beating.

Justice, in war, is frequently convenience. Further, the atrocities of an enemy are always fully exploited, inferring the void of the same in our own troops: We recall a platoon sargeant cutting the jaw of a dead Japanese to ease the removal of gold fillings from the teeth. The Geneva Convention, treatment of prisoners, ha, we recall the tales of the pilots flying Japanese prisoners to Australia, well, half way. They were let out over New Guinea, without a parachute. We recall, the placing of a bounty on every Japanese head brought in by the Dyaks, the head hunters of Borneo. Evidence was presented to prove that the Malayan on trial was a spy. The commando waved Japanese occupation currency taken from the prisoner. This, then, was the conclusive find to spell guilty. We should note that nearly every Australian and American in the area had Japanese occupation currency. Surely, nearly every civilian would have had some of this money as this was the accepted currency for over four years.

Justice, in war, is a mockery. This mockery, as related to soldiers, is probably as it should be. The difficulty arises when soldiers interpret this "law" to the civilian populace.

With due respect to the commando, his official orders were to return suspected spies to headquarters at Sarawak for trial. His unofficial orders were not to "jam the docket."

The day was a hundred years. Time was lavishing each second as a piece of candy lolling on a child's tongue. The sky was now fully overcast, curtaining the earth's horror from the heavens.

Guilty, the prisoner, with hands tied behind him was ordered towards the river. About twenty feet from the bank he was forced to sit on the ground facing the river.

Calmly, oh so calmly, the commando placed the barrel of his carbine against the back of the neck of the Malayan prisoner. "Squeeze them off", we were taught. The shot startled the audience. Quickly as the prisoner fell on his side, the accusing Dyak came forth with a shout and his huge sword held high.

The first blow severed the jugular vein. The sky seemed to redden with the first spurt of blood. Blow, after blow, after blow, after blow. Five hackings to sever the head. We watched almost unbelievingly.

Eight Americans and thirty Australians in this village of savages. Could we have halted this? Worse, did we really want to stop the show?

Our solemnity somehow revived the past. Possibly this is why we bury ourselves in the brain deadening television media. To think is to remember, we do not desire to remember.

Another generation is born. The glamour of the uniform is thrust upon the young mind. History is unbelieving. The television and movies show too few Americans dying. The screen does not transmit the aching loneliness, the quickening fear of nearby death, the cramps and weakening of almost constant diseases which will plague veterans long after they have returned home.

Somehow the knowledge of the hell of war must be transmitted generation to generation. The shrine to wars should include statues of a soldier with a neat bullet hole in his forehead, the burned remains of a flame throwers target, and a corpse with its head lying nearby. Let those that brashly cry for war, visit this shrine. Let all generations know of this shrine. Let those same future generations, in peace, refer to us as the barbaric age.

I have a contribution to this shrine. A one dollar sized piece of JAPANESE OCCUPATIONAL CURRENCY. On it is written 'TAKEN FROM MALAYAN SPY, SHOT BY AUSTRALIAN COMMANDO AND BEHEADED BY A DYAK, July 11, 1945.

J. Ben Lit

An LCM Coxswain Of "C" Company, 593rd EB&SR, T/4 James L. Pullen, tells of the role he and his crew played in the Brunei Bay assault operation.

It was now April 1945, and we had moved our whole unit to the Island of Morotai, in the Dutch East Indies, the staging area for the invasions of Borneo. In the first week in June 1945, Company "C" of the 593rd had their D-day, after traveling from Morotai Island on an LSD (Landing Ship Dock) with our landing craft LCMs. We were launched about five miles offshore from Labuan Island at the mouth of Brunei Bay, Borneo. At dawn the Navy started bombarding the beach with their big guns, there were a dozen destroyers, one large cruiser and other smaller Navy ships. Then converted LSTs carrying rockets advanced toward shore and let go their rockets.

The first wave to go ashore were amphibious tanks, (LVTs, Landing Vehicle, Tracked) from the 593rd. My boat was in the second wave to hit the beach carrying a Matilda tank and an Australian crew. From aerial photos studied in advance, there were to be two pilings on our starboard bow, and there they were. We had a deadfall landing. The tide was out and we were fifty yards from shore but in about two feet of water. So down went the ramp and off went the tank with the Aussies.

By now it was about 11:00 hours. Our next task was to return to a Liberty Ship seven miles out in the ocean and pickup a cargo of fresh water in five gallon cans and return to shore. By the time we arrived back the infantry had landed and the supplies were needed. For the next five or six days we were carrying cargo from ship to shore until docks were repaired and a cargo ship could tie up at shore.

There were Japs in the mountains of Labuan Island and they came down one night and attacked our shore battalion. My landing craft was anchored in the harbor and we ran into shore to see if we were needed. It was pitch dark and our men on shore said they had everything under control so we returned to our anchorage. The next day we found that our men had killed twenty two Japs and we had one man killed and two wounded.

By this time we had troops on Borneo and were busy transporting supplies to Brunei and unloading Liberty Ships along the coast of Sarawak. Aussie troops were moving up the rivers and my boat was loaded with supplies and dispatched up the Lunbong river to Beaufort about forty miles up river. About five miles from Beaufort we were hailed by the Aussie troops and told to wait until they captured the place first before we go further. We could hear the guns from where we were. A gunboat with 50 caliber machine guns and 20 millimeter cannons from "B" Company went past us. A half mile up stream they ran into a Jap ambush on the river. There was a field hospital where we stopped and a few minutes later the gunboat pulled in. The lieutenant on board was shot in the leg and a sargeant was hit in the chest. The Aussie doctor operated on the sargeant right on the deck of the boat. Both were doing all right the next day.

About 22:00 hours that night one of the Aussies came aboard and asked if we would go up the river to pick up some wounded. It was pitch dark and we had to use searchlights to navigate the river. But everything went well and we made two trips and picked up seven wounded men and brought them back to the field hospital. About noon the next day we were headed to Beaufort. They were still fighting there when we arrived there on the other side of town. We unloaded ammo, food and water, about twenty tons of it, and headed back to Brunei.

Another trip I remember well was to Limbang up the Lunbong river. We carried troops far up the river with native Dyaks for guides. The stream went to the foot of the mountains. Some people on shore waved to us and seemed very excited. We picked them up and it was a Chinese doctor and his family who had been hiding in the hills since the Japs had invaded the island. They had been living off the land but were in good condition. We tied up to the shore at a place called Yukon and waited for the patrol to return. They got back late the next day and I was surprised to see the Dyaks carrying Jap heads they had acquired. These people were headhunters and now the Japs were fair game. I am glad they were on our side.

A Banzai Charge Is Remembered By Those Men Of Company "B" Who Participated In The Attack.

The following account of this attack was told to a RAMP correspondent by a former member of "B" Company, S/Sargeant John Sharchuck.

On 21 June 1945, at 04:00 hours, "B" Company of the 593rd EB&SR, located at Labuan Island, in Brunei Bay, Borneo, were attacked by Japanese soldiers.

A group of eighty or more Japanese troops broke through the perimeter and attacked the amphibious engineer area. The Japanese suicidal raiding party infiltrated through the perimeter about 04:45 hours attacking the company area. The two guards challenged the approaching party and fired on them. When the challenge was not complied with the guards withdrew and warned the company personnel of the attack. The enemy had a concealed approach to the "B" Company area and also had the cover of trucks parked at the side of the road. The enemy fired into the tents, set fire to the seats of the trucks in an effort to disable them. They also caused flat tires on the vehicles.

S/Sargeant Danny Caparella noted that the Japs made two big mistakes: one, they set fire to "B" Company's laundry tent, thus illuminating the whole area and their leader, Captain Okuyama, who spoke perfect English, yelled out, "Don't shoot, Australian patrol coming through, "but the Captain held up a saber, which was the second mistake. Private Wallace Curtis challenged Okuyama, and the Captain ran his saber through Curtis' stomach. Curtis died days later. It was a soldier named Twiddy that gave the alarm to wake the men in the tents. The warning came through the men's tents that the Japanese were attacking. It was a Banzai attack.

Before you knew it, all hell broke loose. Company "B" was hit very hard. There was shooting and grenades going off all over the area. Men were scrambling for positions in their T-shirt and skivvies. Half of the time the men of the company did not know if they were being shot at by their own men or by the Japs. The Japs came through the perimeter which was in the rear of the maintenance area. The action started there and spread throughout the encampment. The Japs attacked the tents, throwing grenades and shooting wildly. Four men of company "B" were killed and five others were wounded. The men of the company were literally caught with their pants down. Sergeant Caparella was lying in his tent in a prone position and his tent was on the shore road side. He spotted a Jap sneaking around from the direction of Headquarters company area, which was about thirty yards from his tent. The Jap was in a slouched position outside his tent with a rifle and bayonet ready to attack. Caparella shot twice at the Jap and killed him. When daybreak came and the fighting was over, Caparella looked over the body of the soldier that he had killed. One shot had hit the Jap in the stomach and the other shot was right between the eyes. The men of the company took a count of the slain enemy and it totaled forty eight that had gone to join their ancestors. After the fighting was over a Japanese Plan of Attack, prepared by Captain Okuyama was found and translated: it stated that the Japs planned to kill all of company "B." The Japanese officer, seeing that his forces were being destroyed instead of victorious, as he had planned, committed honorable Hara-Kiri, disemboweling himself. Pictures of the dead Japanese soldiers are shown here to demonstrate the futility and waste of lives that result from warfare. (See page 70)

After the battle was over, the dead enemy soldiers were laid out so the troops could see their enemy, then a burial detail took the Japanese soldiers to the cemetery. The remainder of the morning after the battle was over, was used to improve the security of the encampment area. T/4 Goldschmidt was killed during the Banzai attack. He had left his helmet outside the tent and in trying to retrieve it during the attack he was felled by a Japanese hand grenade, just outside his tent.

A comment from T/Sargeant DeBlaise concerning the enemy soldier shot by Caparella during the attack. DeBlaise said, "I was just three feet from the Jap soldier, when I heard Caparella say, I think I got one of the bastards." I knew that Jap was headed for me and I didn't have my gun with me, I had lost it in the scuffle to get out of the tent. You know I owe Caparella my life! The raiding party set fire to the laundry tent and this in turn ignited four drums of gasoline, illuminating the area and providing light for the company to return fire. Three company men, T/4 Goldschmidt, T/5 Venorsky and Private Curtis were fatally wounded. Lieutenant Whitney was fatally wounded trying to evacuate the wounded men to the aid station. T/4 Lord and T/Benham were seriously wounded and two more were slightly wounded. In the morning after the hostilities ceased, thirty four Japanese were found dead.

The "pocket" mentioned in the RAMP story of 24 June 1945 was an area just north of the company "B," encampment area. It was a small densely wooded jungle area where the Japanese went into when the Australian troops cleared the island of most of the enemy. The troops in the "pocket" were desperate and they knew that it was just a matter of time until the Australians would overrun the "pocket" area and kill them or capture them. They were not ready for either of these alternatives to take place. For the past eighteen days the Australians had been pouring artillery fire into their last refuge. The Australians knew they were there and Australian Matilda tanks and troops were moving into the "pocket" area from the southwest and Australian infantry and artillery were already in position 'on the north and east of the "pocket" area. These remaining enemy troops had nothing to loose. They chose a dark night and picked their way through the dense mangrove swamps and made their way down a dry stream bed that meandered near the company "B" encampment area. There were reasons to believe their objective was first to overcome company "B", gain access to the boat pier, manage to obtain a landing craft and escape from the island to the mainland.

The 24 June 1945 issue of RAMP carried a story entitled "Where Were The Japs?" It was regarding the negligible resistance of a recent amphibious landing in the Netherlands East Indies. The assault later advanced to the point where it was understood that the only remaining Japanese were in a pocket at the other end of the island. The Japanese evidently knew nothing of this understanding, because one morning about 04:00 hours T/4 Lord couldn't sleep. The morning was pitch black and the weather was dry. Lord had been relieved of guard duty at 04:00 hours and had not quite become comfortable enough to go to sleep with Pfc. Twiddy ran screaming through the company area, "Japs! Japs! Everybody get up!"

Twiddy had been guarding the left flank. The Japs had infiltrated down a narrow stream through the infantry perimeter and had slugged the guard on the right flank of the company. Just across the road towards the perimeter sat the company vehicles. A little way on the other side of the vehicles the company had set up its laundry tent. The laundry tent immediately turned into an inferno when the Japanese threw dry leaves among the gasoline cans and set fire to the tinder. The enemy troops then punctured the vehicle tires and tried to destroy them by fire, but the damage was only sight.

The Japs then made a combination flanking and frontal assault on the area and were firing their weapons through the company area and heaving grenades into the tents along the road. The Japs were jumping over oil barrels trying to break through the company lines crying "Banzai! Banzai! Honorable Nipponese!"

In the Motor Pool tent which was one of the tents in the first row, Pfc. Gordon was the first Amphib to awaken. He could hear the bullets ripping through his mosquito bar. A peanut can on the table was hit squarely and the fatal bullet only slightly toasted the peanuts inside. Gordon fell to the floor for safety and crawled around the awakened Pvt. Robinson, then tried unsuccessfully to arouse T/4 Santos and got him out of his sack. Finally when Gordon and Robinson felt that Santos was sufficiently awake, they took off. Santos, still half awake was looking for his glasses and asked if anyone could find them. The figure standing with him in the tent answered him in Japanese. Finally realizing the situation, Santos literally flew from the tent without his spectacles.

The company officers, T/5 Harrington, S/Sargeant Hamilton, and several other Amphibs defied the attacking Japanese by going into the tents that were bearing the brunt of the assault to evacuate the wounded to the officers tents. They were just behind and to the right of the first row of tents and these were used as a collecting point for the wounded.

The enemy fired the Motor Pool twice and both times Acting First Sargeant Gardner ran from cover and smothered the flames. The Japs seemed to be everywhere at once, for the moment. Behind the company area was another road and across this road and to the right of the Amphibious Engineers was an Amphibious Tank company. The Amphib tanks had been so deployed that either approach on the road (beach road) could be adequately covered by their 50 caliber machine guns. The gunners on the tank's right flank noticed what appeared to be a patrol boldly marching down the road. They challenged and the patrol answered, "Don't shoot we are an Allied patrol." A glint of light gleamed momentarily from the surface of a saber and the Japs were promptly annihilated on the spot. Meanwhile the gunner on the unit's left flank could see the advancing Japs outlined against the fiery background of the blazing laundry tent. Their 50 caliber guns slaughtered everything in their path. The Brigade Amphibs were plenty thankful to their Amphibian brothers for their assistance.

Some of the enemy troops had bombs strapped to their backs and at least two of these little men were blown to bits when their bombs were smashed by the tank gunners. Apparently the primary objective of the enemy's ill fated mission was to destroy a newly constructed pier below the Amphibs company area. At least one Jap got almost to the pier but was caught in a cross fire by some Engineer Maintenance men and some sailors.

An officer from 1st Battalion Headquarters had volunteered to drive a truck into the midst of the attack to evacuate the wounded. Seeing the truck sitting there, T/4 Sauer who was under the impression that casualties were in the vehicle, ran out of cover and climbed into the truck and somehow managed to get the vehicle safely away from danger.

T/5 Beitzel ran from his tent. He heard a bolt click twice and automatically realized it was a Jap. He yelled, "It's a Jap, shoot the son of a bitch." The Jap threw a hand grenade and attempted to flee but didn't get very far. Three Amphibs argued as to who would get credit for sending the honorable one to his bloody end. Beitzel was not injured.

Another son of heaven met his end but appropriately he made his last stand at the Amphib Maintenance men's latrine. T/5 Krajiceck of that unit was extremely fortunate. A saber-swinging Jap chased him out of bed, sans clothing, and managed to carve only a shallow cross on Krajiceck's back.

The smoke of battle cleared away approximately a half hour after daylight. More Japs were found lurking in culverts, beside logs, behind parts of war weary buildings and other debris. At least forty two dead "Honorable Nipponese" had been sent on the straight and narrow to Jap heaven. Although the cooks had defended the kitchen building successfully, all the atabrine bottles were smashed and the pots and pans had become slightly the worse for wear and tear. That didn't make much difference because the Amphibs weren't much hungry anyway.

In a glowing tribute to his commanding officer, Captain Cavanaugh, a sargeant from his company made the following statement. "A lot of men would have been killed if it were not for him, his coolness and leadership under fire proved too much for the "Japs".

The following is a copy of the Japanese Banzai Attack order issued by Captain Okuyama to the soldiers of his unit just prior to the attack on Company "B".

BANZAI CHARGE ON LABUAN ISLAND

The orders for the final assault on the Beach
Maintenance Area at Labuan Island, Borneo on the night
(20/21) June 1945 have been captured and the following
is a translation:

PENETRATION ORDER

1.   The force will execute its last assault from the
direction of Weapon Pit Barracks and Force Guard Post.

ALLOCATION OF UNITS

2.   First Assault Unit, commanded by Captain OKUYAMA.
Hq Yanagi Unit 3 Coy. 4 Coy M.P. Unit. Second
Assault Unit First Lieutenant ISHIKAWA. Working Unit
Intendence Det. Ordnance Det. SAKAI Unit First Coy and
Weapons Unit.
3.   The First Assault Unit will break though the enemy
lines from the Force Guard Post and will carry out the
final attack with the harbour area as objective.
4.   The Second Assault Unit will break through the
enemy lines from the vicinity of Guard Barracks passing
in the vicinity of the Navy OZAKI Unit Barracks, and
from the area of the airfield will advance to the
harbour area:
5.   Those who are seriously wounded will dedicate
themselves and those who are slightly wounded will
complete their Spiritual Training and remain in their
positions inflicting as many casualties as possible.

6.   TIME OF ASSEMBLY AND SORTIE
To-morrow 20th June. Various Assault Units. Complete
Assembly at 2200 hours. Leave the said area at 2210
hours.
Captain OKUYAMA

Japanese soldiers killed in the Banzai charge of June 21, 1945 on Labuan Island. Photo courtesy of Ernest Paquette. It was first used in his book.

Another view of the enemy after the Banzai charge on Labuan Island. This was the final Banzai charge of World War II. Note: the important point of this picture is to show that Americans and Australians fought together on Labuan Island and other parts of Borneo.

A Japanese officer (Capt. Okuyama) who committed Hara Kiri after the unsuccessful Japanese Banzai charge on Labuan Island, June 21, 1945. Photo was used in Ernest Paquette's book "Our business is Beachheads." The photo is through courtesy of Ernest Paquette.

Another photograph of the dead enemy after the fatal Banzai charge on Labuan Island. Australian soldiers looking at their foe. Photo courtesy of Mrs. Harold (Ruth) Killoran.

A Dyak (headhunter) holding the severed head of a Japanese soldier he had killed. Labuan Island, Borneo, July 1945. Photo courtesy of John W. Cunningham.

The following is provided to describe the natives of Borneo that were very effective in fighting the Japanese that occupied their homeland and robbed them of much of their foodstuff to feed the Japanese Army during their occupation in World War II.

The people of Borneo were headhunters and were feared by many. The different spelling of their name is as follows; Dyak or Dayak or the Dutch spelling of Dajak. These are the spellings of the name of a non-Muslim indigenous people living in the southern and western portions of Borneo the area of the island now known as Kalimantan. There are several groups of these people, the Kayan that inhabit central and eastern Borneo; the Nagaju or Land Dyaks of southern Borneo; and in southwestern Borneo and Sarawak there are the Iban or Sea Dyaks. In reality the Sea Dyaks are not sea people but they are riverine and hill dwellers. Their economy is based on dry land rice farming. There is another group of Dyaks that live near the coast of Sarawak who have maintained their identity as Dyaks and they have embraced the Muslim religion.

This group no longer lives in longhouses but now live in individual homes much like the Malay people.

Dyaks are generally riverine people and live in longhouse communities usually consisting of two or three hundred persons. The family is the basic unit, children remain with the family until they are married and boys marry into a family outside their longhouse. Among some of the Dyaks there is no class distinction but among others. there are three classes, the upper class made up of family and relatives of the village chief, the middle class consists of members of the village or longhouse and the lowest are the captives of war.

The source of subsistence of the Dyaks is from rice farming, hunting for game animals and from fishing. Their weapons consist of a sword, spear and blow gun.

Most conform to an animistic or polytheistic religion. This form of religion is generally concerned with the well being of the tribe, the raising of good rice crops and the ability to cure the illness of the people. Bad forces must be paid off and good ones must be rewarded with gifts.

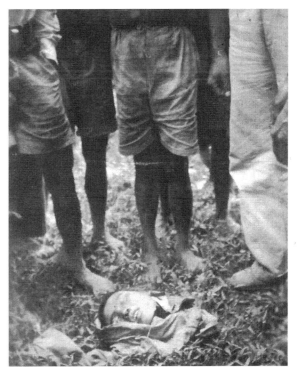

Dyaks standing over the severed head of a Japanese soldier that they had killed. The Allies encouraged headhunting on Borneo—as long as it was the enemies' heads that they cut off. Photo courtesy of John W. Cunningham.

71

The longhouse is a peaked roof building raised some twenty feet above the ground on hardwood tree trunks as posts. A corridor along one side leads to the inner family compartments or bileks and divides the house lengthwise. Steps or ladders are used for an entrance. Near the entrance to the longhouse the heads of enemies taken in battle are placed for display.

The Dyaks were a valuable ally to the troops fighting in Borneo during World War II. They were headhunters by nature and were most happy to help troops dispose of the Japanese invaders. Military personnel were parachuted into the area dominated by the Dyaks and they organized the natives into fighting units to hunt down and destroy the enemy in the jungle areas. The Japanese demanded that the Dyaks provide the Japanese Army with large amounts of rice.

A Dyak holding a Japanese soldier's head that he had cut off.

A Dyak "smoking" another Japanese head (note the head hanging behind the head-hunter). The Dyaks hated the Japanese.

A Dyak holding a rope-bag full of the heads of Japanese soldiers on Borneo.

A posed photograph of a Dyak chieftain on Brunei Bay, Borneo. This photograph came from a pre-war postal card sold to tourists on Borneo. Photo courtesy of Mrs. Armand (Laurette) Gosselin.

Above: The clock tower on Labuan Island before the bombing. The tower was presented to the people of Labuan by Chee Shee Chang, a Chinese businessman. The houses and stores in the picture were destroyed by allied bombing. See right for the remains of the clock tower and Victoria Town Square after the bombing. Top photo courtesy of Robert Boddy. Photo to the right courtesy of Welton Stein.

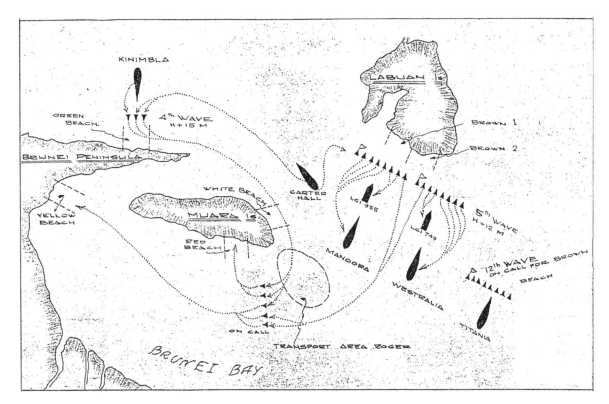

A detailed map of Brunei Bay showing Labuan and Muara Islands and the various landings. The Australians landed on Muara Island and Brunei itself, while the 593rd (1st platoon, Company "B") landed on Labuan Island.

The following are the remembrances of Faye Clarke, an Australian Nurse who served with the Australian Forces on Labuan Island during World War II.

Orders finally came that we were needed abroad. We were given cholera and tetanus injections and sent to Cairns, then a scruffy seaport full of Americans, to board the Hospital Ship Manunda. The HS Manunda was very comfortable, she had the scars from the bombs dropped near her when the Japanese shelled Darwin. We got as far as Morotai and were taken ashore as Japan had declared open warfare on our hospital ships. We were there about three weeks. We camped in a coconut plantation with those wretched things crashing near tents day and night.

Aboard the Manunda, Thursday 19 July 1945. No mail for the 2/6th and we all disembark tomorrow at 09:00 hours for a two weeks stay on Morotai Island, it seems our boys of the unit have gone on. Padre Boof Beythein learned of Frank's death, having been killed on Balikpapan some nine days ago.

It is 09:30 hours and we are dancing on deck when the raid alert went and so we blacked out and stood by with life jackets. We pack, for tomorrow we go "terra firma" again.

Friday 20 July 1945. We rose and packed by 08:00 hours and assembled on the promenade deck for disembarkation from 09:00 hours onwards. We drew in at the wharf just recently constructed by Aussie Engineers.

We were taken by truck to the 2/9th A.S.H. along a three mile route on either side thick with jungle and here there was an army camp of American Air Force Station. The hospital which is situated beneath a coconut plantation is most attractive under those tall graceful palms towering high above us. We had morning tea awaiting us by 2/9th A.A.M.W.S. It was terribly hot, very humid, and rain was threatening. The water is acute so we will all appreciate rain, however, it rains daily we are told.

The Japanese surrender plane. Photo courtesy of Robert Boddy.

Another Japanese surrender plane. Photo courtesy of Robert Boddy.

Australian soldiers on the airfield at Labuan. Note the Japanese standing behind the group and the pilot sitting on top of the pilot's escape hatch with his hands behind his neck in surrender. Photo courtesy of Robert Boddy.

Another view of the same surrender plane, with the Japanese pilot coming out of the escape hatch while Australian diggers watch. Photo courtesy of Robert Boddy.

Australian planes on the tarmack at Labuan airstrip. Photo courtesy of Deward Offutt.

To drink the water is distasteful as one could imagine, even in tea and with tinned sweetened milk. I think this where I give it up and take black tea.

Airplanes, never is the air clear of them, day and night, squads of them go over to do their bombing on Borneo at Balikpapan. The sky at night is a mass of searchlights. The hospital ship Manunda still sits off. We are just across the way from the 2/5th A.S.H. and they are right on the beach so we are able to swim, it is nice, but we must wear shoes for the coral surface is very cutting. The water is warm and horrid.

Our lives are quite comfortable considering we are here for only a two-week stay. All in large tents that accommodate thirty, dirt floors of course, but we have a mess and showers. Lavies pit system and all very pally with just a small division between. The showers are terrific and one often finds the body all soaked and off goes the water. This happens many times a day.

It soon became time to leave Morotai Island and proceed to our original destination, Brunei Bay and Labuan Island, Borneo. We departed Morotai Island aboard ship, around the top of Borneo, and on the way called at Zamboango, in the southern Philippines, and then on to Labuan. Our hospital, the 2/6th Australian General Hospital, was on Labuan Island. We were supposed to arrive July 1945 but due to the interference of the Japanese, we did not arrive until early August. There was another Australian hospital at Sandakan and of course the Casualty Clearing Stations (C.C.S.) also treated some of the lads. There was a large U.S. Force south of us where the invasion took place. We received a few casualties and soldiers suffering from jaundice, dysentery and malaria.

We did once we were established, nurse only a few casualties from the invasion. Our main objective was to gather up the boys who had been held in Java and other islands who were too ill to move back to Aussie. You probably know what a dreadful time they had. These lads were wrecked mentally, physically, having been beaten and starved. So we were on Labuan till the end of December 1945.

They all suffered from malnutrition and their limbs were like sticks, no hairs, ulcers, skin like brown paper impossible to inject as there was no flesh, eyes which told their own story. We had to feed them two hourly nourishments as they could not tolerate a decent meal. I could pick up these grown men in my arms and carry them as one would carry a baby.

The men would lie in their beds, eighty to a ward. They would fall asleep and often when you awoke them they would jump up ready to defend themselves, then apologize and weep. I do admit after a while when I was tired, shocked and not very brave, I found it difficult not to weep along with them, but at night in my tent was a different story. Battle casualties in the Middle East was horrible, but these lads were well fed, fit and healthy men, these poor boys were broken in body, mind and spirit. We truly hated the Japs for what they had done to our boys. We had a couple in our hospital as patients, they had tried to commit Hara-Kiri with a table knife, they were given blood transfusions and lived. The POWs were very cross that we were keeping them alive, a double guard had to be put on the ward to protect the Jap prisoners. Of course the only reason the Japs were kept alive was so they could give evidence at the war trials, they were later shot, we were told.

I remember we had an annex off the ward, half way along, forty patients at either end. Well, as we came out of the ward through the annex these monkeys would sit above the door and lean down and pull our veils off, and as we tried to retrieve them they spit on us. They would also raid the pantry and steal the malted milk or extra nourishment we had prepared for the boys. The Red Cross were wonderful, they sent malted milk and etc., but the savior was vegemite. We would make a broth out of it, mash it in their vegetables, into stew, anything to get it into their systems. Any wonder to this day I despise Japs and swear by vegemite.

Life for us was not easy, many nights we would have a tropical downpour and our tent pegs would give way and we would have to get out and bash them back in, only to repeat it many times more each night. A wet soggy tent falling on one is not a pleasant bed mate. Camp life was basic, the water was chlorinated, the food was awful greasy bully beef stew for breakfast, we miss our pineapples and all the other lovely fruit we had in Queensland. There was no entertainment excepting Gracie Fields who gave a concert and stayed overnight sleeping in the Sisters lines. My tent mate and I had to take her tea and biscuits and to see that she was ok. My tent mates were Beryl Followes and Doreen Chatel. Monty, Gracie's large Italian husband, had to sleep in the MO's lines and when ever they were in sight

Tony Szarnicki standing by a P-51 Mustang fighter plane at the airstrip on Labuan Island, September 1945. Photo courtesy of John W. Cunningham.

The beer shipment has arrived! Photo courtesy of Tony DeBlasie.

Officers shower on Labuan Island, September 1945. Left to right: Lt. John G. Orr and Captain Cavanaugh. Photo courtesy of Lt. John W. Cunningham.

of one another, it was "Monty" and "Gracie" and kisses were thrown. For weeks afterwards when we would see other staff members we would call and throw a kiss, it was real fun.

We were so yellow from atabrine which we took for malaria and here was Gracie in her lovely black evening frock and her beautiful peaches and cream complexion, we were so envious. Thousands came to her concert, the lads would call what they wanted her to sing. During the performance there was a tremendous downpour, Gracie kept on singing, she of course was protected from the rain and we all stood in the downpour enjoying every minute of it.

When we were posted night duty we tried to get a swim in during the day; unfortunately, the tide was out during this period which meant we had to walk a long way out to reach deep water. The heat often made us feel sick, it was just too hot and very unpleasant. I was very fortunate that I did not fall sick while service aboard apart from measles at Gaza, sand fly fever in Queensland and prickly heat in Borneo, nothing kept me off duty for any length of time. I had the odd boil but that was a nuisance more than debilitating. Before leaving Labuan the War Cemetery personnel were preparing to bring bodies from outlying areas to create a decent resting place for the fallen soldiers.

While at Labuan we had the satisfaction of seeing the lads that had been in the Japanese prison camps improved in health and spirit, and now many of them were fit to return home on the hospital ship. The oil wells along the beach were still burning when we left, the Japs had set fire to them along with the rubber plantations, this was in keeping with their scorched earth policy. Christmas time 1945, several dozen of us girls returned on the ship "Wanganella" with many sick lads. Also on board were civilians who had been POWs in Singapore, the Red Cross was caring for them. Many of them were English expatriates. I remember one lady with two children whose husband had been taken away by the Japs and she had not heard from him, she was hoping the Red Cross would find him. The civilians had been roughly treated but not tortured like our boys had. The boys received a wonderful reception, but very sad. When the ship arrived in Sydney, the "Wanganella" then traveled onto Melbourne and then to Tasmania.

I enjoyed two weeks of leave and returned to Melbourne to hopefully a discharge. But Major

Appleford had other ideas for me, she wished me to go to Japan with the Occupation Force, so this lowly Corporal told the Major; no way would I step foot on Japanese soil after the way they treated our boys. According to her it was all over and I was to think it over. I went on the troop train in the R.A.P. to Sydney and Melbourne each week and every few weeks I would go see the Major and each time I was told she valued my five years in the service and couldn't do without me. She told me that she would make me a lieutenant but I must go to Japan. After five months of this rot I told her I would walk away, forfeit my deferred pay, and I meant it. My tent mate and I planned to go to New Zealand, as we had twice planned to meet her cousin who was in the New Zealand army and who we had tried to meet in Beirut and Cairo.

I finally got my discharge with a lecture as long as your arm about loyalty to the service after five years. I was not amused. One year and one day later I married Beryl's cousin and we have lived happily ever after.

The following is some of the history of the Voluntary Aid Detachments. The tradition of women serving as Aids to the professional staffs of the Australian Army Medical Corps and the Australian Army Nursing Service of Military Hospitals was established during World War I.

In peace time between the two wars, members of Detachments of Voluntary Aids worked in hospitals and convalescent homes. Many VAs were members of the Nursing Division of St. John's Brigade, others worked with the Australian Red Cross Society.

After the outbreak of war in 1939, members of Voluntary Aid Detachments, all of whom held First Aid and Home Nursing Certificates, were called on to assist in military hospitals throughout Australia, and many did so, working full time in a purely voluntary capacity and providing their own uniforms, until early in 1941, in order to free men for active service, it was decided that the VADs should be enlisted for Army Service in Military Hospitals in Australia.

The Australian General Hospitals were serving in the Middle East when the War Cabinet agreed to a request for female personnel to replace males in some areas of the Medical Services. On 8 August 1941, the Department of Army announced that the Military Board had approved the employment of female members of the Voluntary Aid Detachments in Military Hospitals with the AIF overseas.

It was initially intended to send four drafts of two hundred enlisted from all States, to the Middle East. However, because of Japan's entry into the war and consequent threats to Australia, only one contingent left Australia on 1 November 1941. The main body embarked on the "Queen Mary" at Sydney, the remainder, from western Australia were to join the ship in Fremantle.

On arrival in the Middle East the Voluntary Aids spent nearly two months in a staging camp in Palestine and were then posted, in approximately equal numbers to the 2/1st Army General Hospital, (later the 2/6th Army General Hospital) at Gaza Ridge. In January 1943, they returned to Australia with the Australian 9th Division and many members saw further service in the Southwest Pacific theater of Operations.

THOSE LITTLE YANKEE BARGES

They landed us on the beachhead
When we made our assault on Lae;
It was their first taste of battle
When they took us in that day.
They didn't heed the bullets
Or the bombers angry roar,
They stood at the wheels of the barges
And drove them to the shore;
And they backed us up and helped us
On the long drive up the coast.
"We'll get supplies and ammo through
Without fail", was their boast.
Into little bays the Japs had held
Not very long before.
They nosed their little barges in
And drove them at the shore!
They brought our mail and rations up
And put them on the sand.
When the Zeros tried to stop them
Their gun crews took a hand.

In wet and stormy weather
With the crew of three in each,
Those Yankees got their barges through
And landed them on the beach!
We loaded on our wounded
And they took them back to base.
Then loaded up with stores once more,
To the battle front they would race.
They did just what we asked of them,
No man could e'er do more,
The Yanks with their little barges
Plying from shore to shore!
And when the war is over,
T'wil live in our memories;
How the Yankee boat battalion
Conquered the Coral Seas.
The Japs, too, will remember,
Remember forever more;
Those little Yankee barges
A'heading for his shore!

This poem appeared in an Australian Newspaper as a tribute to the United States Amphibious Engineer Forces who worked with the Australian Forces in New Guinea. The Australians recognized the Amphibious Engineers as one of the finest of American Allies. Some of the Diggers went home on leave telling stories of the friendship and camaraderie between the Amphibious Engineers and some of Australia's most famous divisions.

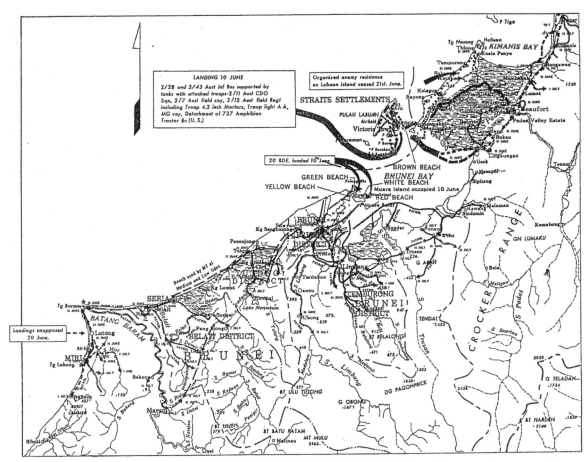

Map of Brunei Bay and surroundings.

When General MacArthur sailed on the U.S.S. Boise, he left the ship at Brunei Bay to watch the landings of the U.S. and Australian troops. He was in danger all the time with Japanese rifle fire all around him and his party. When the Aussies killed two Japs, MacArthur went to examine one of the dead enemy's cartridge boxes. At that instant, a photographer who was taking MacArthur's picture was shot in the shoulder by an enemy sniper. One of the officers in the party convinced the General to return to the ship. A dead General would be of little use in holding the entire Southwest Pacific campaign together.

General Douglas MacArthur congratulates Captain W.M. Downes (Commander of the U.S.S. Boise), after receiving a gold star in lieu of a second award of the Legion of Merit (Brunei Bay, Borneo, Netherlands East Indies). Photo by Quon, 11 June 1945. U.S. Army Signal Corps. Photo.

OFFICERS: Left to right: J. Orr, 3rd Platoon: J. Cavanaugh. 2nd Platoon; E. Zaloom, Executive Officer; R. Wood, Commanding Officer; W. Parker, Navigation Officer; A. Szarnicki, 1st Platoon; and Lt. Simpson, Signal Officer.

OFFICERS AND NON-COMS OF COMPANY "C"

NON-COMS: Left to right: R. Boddy, G. Gabrielson, W. Thompson, A. Orr, L. Lindsey and J.C. Goss. Standing next to the 593rd Brag Board on Borneo, 1945.

First Platoon Company B 593rd EBSR
Labuan Island, Borneo Sept. 1945

Row 1. (bottom), left to right: Dewitt, Helige, Radzewicz, Murdecki, Jenneman, Lt.
Cunningham, Capt. Cavanaugh, Snoots, Reddin, Atcheley, Chapman and
Comer.
Row 2. Smeland, Curtis, Nazar, Narefski, Sparrow, Bieszka, Sebek, Stelmachowski,
Paquette, Clark, Krygier and Kemper.
Row 3. Jaskella, Farris, Throckmorton, Kreuzeberger, Hinkson, Palmieri, Moran,
Richter, Mullin, Muroff, Angeloni and Baker.
Row 4. McMurchy, Harvey, Rose, Chilcote, Schrader, Feldlaufer, Freeman,
Horinbein, Phelps, Largen, Graack, Hickey, Guldseth, DePrete, Taylor and
Thomas.

Tents of Company "C"
men pitched on Labuan
Island, Borneo, June
1945. The two men
holding the Japanese
flag: left to right:
James Sheehan and
Mike Harmon. Photo
courtesy of Mike
Harmon.

CHAPTER 7
Balikpapan

The last of the Allied Assault Operations in Borneo was at Balikpapan, the location of a major oil refinery of the Dutch Shell Oil Company. The operation was originally planned for execution on 22 May 1945, but orders were changed due to conflicts in the Tarakan and Brunei Bay assault landings. Later the date was set for 28 June, but due to delays in moving troops to the staging area the date was changed to 1 July 1945.

Troops involved would be the 7th Australian Division, "A" company of the 593rd Engineer Boat & Shore Regiment, one company of the 672nd Amphibious Tractor Battalion and a Detachment of the 1463rd Engineer Maintenance company. Balikpapan was located on a large sheltered harbor, a town of importance, containing modern refineries and industrial plants for the processing and shipping of petroleum products. The town contained a Japanese garrison of 4,500 troops with well fortified positions with gun emplacements, pillboxes, barbed wire entanglements and offshore obstacles on all logical landing beaches. The landings were made on the beaches to the northeast of the harbor entrance. There were three designated beaches, Red, Yellow and Green. H-hour was set for 09:00 hours and the initial assault waves would be taken ashore by LVTs (Landing Vehicles Tracted) and by Navy LCVPs (Landing Craft Vehicle Personnel). "A" company landing craft went ashore immediately following the initial waves.

On 24 June 1945, the convoy assembled at Morotai Island, moved out at 1515 hours and formed into cruising positions off the northwest coast of the Halmahera Island. LSMs and LSTs towed 21 LCMs and one picket boat. The LSD "Carter Hall" carried 18 LCMs and 2 "J" boats, in the well deck and the utility boat and the maintenance boat on its top deck. The AKA deck loaded 6 LCMs and 21 LCMs and 1 picket boat were towed by LSMs and LSTs.

A typical amphibious operation was as described in the War Diary of 2nd Lieutenant James Pounds, Operations Officer of "A" company of the 593rd Engineer boat & Shore Regiment, who was assigned as the Control Officer Afloat for all company craft in the Balikpapan operation.

"A" company operations at Red Beach on Morotai Island are scheduled to cease on the 15th June 1945, and training for the operation at Balikpapan, Borneo to start on the 17th of June. The "dry run" will be on the east side of Morotai, practice D-day and H-hour will be 09:00 hours 22 June, the landing practice went well nothing unusual occurred. The LCMs were not loaded back on the AKAs and all proceeded to the anchorage at Loengee Loengee Island in convoy, the M9A1 leading and all craft arrived at the anchorage at 18:00 hours 22 June. All crafts were refueled and tied up to their respective ships. The LSD "Carter Hall" was reloaded and also the AKAs, all in readiness to depart on the OBOE II operation at Balikpapan. My boat the M9A0, the Control Boat for the operation, was towed by LSM 42, a very nice skipper and I think we will have a good trip. A Japanese bombing raid occurred at 03:00 hours 23 June, not much damage, just a few stray bombs here and there.

We departed on the real thing at 14:00 hours 24 June. I rode in the M9A0 with the crew and we had good chow even had a case of canned turkey which our Allies, the US Navy, provided. The sea was very calm until we entered the passage to the north end of the Makassar Straits. We were joined here by the Naval Task Force, one carrier and several cruisers. The whole convoy consisted of one hundred sixty craft, including US Navy, US Army, British, Australian and Dutch.

We arrived off Balikpapan at 03:00 hours on 1 July 1945, we cut loose from our tow and proceeded to the rendezvous area off Green Beach. All assault Waves were forming at daylight under the smoke of the burning oil tanks onshore and from the terrific naval bombardment. A Naval vessel had been shelling the area back of the beaches and along the mountain ridges constantly since our arrival in the area. The Air Corps and Navy Planes are saturation bombing the same areas. The bombing is so heavy and intense it is a wonder that anything is standing in the area. The huge fires and billowing smoke was visible for fifty miles on our approach. The water inshore is covered with a thick layer of oil.

An aerial view of the bombing results by the allies on the oil depot at Balikpapan, Borneo, prior to the allied invasion of July 1, 1945. US Army Signal Corps. Photo courtesy of James A. Pounds.

The first wave landed 0910 hours 1 July, one LCM was blown up on the beach by a depth charge and all the crew were saved. Every LCM was in operation, what a job, keeping all the orders for LCMs filled. A very rough beach sand and surf. We worked all night and the bombardment is still going on. The Navy lost two mine sweepers the first day to free floating mines. The harbor and the beach area here at Balikpapan had been mined by the British, the Dutch, the Japanese and the US Navy during the past three years. There were tethered mines, magnetic mines and underwater booby traps wired to obstacles on the surface. The Colonel and the Major from battalion spent the night aboard the J9A2. One LCM was blown up

due to a sea mine, the crew was saved, at 14:00 HOURS 2 July, another LCM was lost to sea mines, and at 18:00 hours 4 July, another LCM was lost to mines, but all the crew were saved. One LCM lost due to mines at 1830 hours 5 July, all the crew were lost. The M9A0 Control Boat was the target of two five inch Japanese artillery shells fired from a cave in the hills overlooking the beach area on 6 July. There were two direct hits through the stern and the shells impacted into the starboard engine. Lieutenant Sherlock and four enlisted men were wounded and evacuated by the Navy. What a wallop those things pack. We were very fortunate it did not hit amidship in the radio room. We transferred to the M9G3 to carry on the Control

Operations. At 24:00 hours 4 July, a submarine surfaced in the small boat anchorage and shelled some of the landing craft. The submarine was later destroyed by a Navy cruiser.

We moved the Maintenance Section and "A" company headquarters within the harbor at 14:00 hours 7 July. Lieutenant Kluba's boat, then Colonel Emerson's boat and they were the first Allied craft to enter the harbor since January 1942. I was first ashore at 10:00 hours 11 July. It was quite a treat to be ashore after three weeks of day and night on the boats. Moved ashore at 08:00 hours 22 July, and set up operations on Green Beach. Moved to the inner harbor at Brown Beach 07:00 hours 24 July, a nice set up. The company area was moved from Brown Beach to Banoe Hoeke, a ship yard, a very nice area for company operations. There was quiet water for an anchorage for the LCMs and adequate docks for loading and unloading supplies. Now that the beaches had been secured there was not a great deal of activity, just routine supply and recon missions. Lieutenant Kluba's third platoon was on river patrol and resupply for the Australian troops inland. We captured a Japanese ship and several small craft. Sunk one gun boat near Riko Village. Patrols to Soembodjia and the Koeti river mouth. M9G3 was shot up at Soembawa 14:00 hours on 4 August, three crew members were wounded. The gunboat had taken a direct hit from a Japanese 25 millimeter on the forward 37 millimeter gun. The men were evacuated to the States. Lieutenant Hamilton and Lieutenant Tallman arrived 14:00 hours 14 August. I received orders to report to Regimental Headquarters, APO 73, Batangas, Luzon, The Philippines, at 18:00 hours 18 August 1945. Departed Balikpapan 14:00 hours 20 August on board His Majesty's Australian Ship the"Junee," a caravel; arrived Morotai Island 06:00 hours 24 August; departed Morotai 08:00 hours 25 August for Clark Field; departed Clark Field for Nichols Field 16:00 hours 25 August and arrived 18:00 hours 25 August. Spent the night at the 593rd Engineer Boat & Shore Regiment camp located on Dewey Boulevard in Manila departed Manila for Batangas at 14:00 hours 26 August, by jeep, arriving there at 18:00 hours 26 August 1945.

Met the old crowd, sure was good to see them again. I learned from the Regimental Commander that I was to be the Boat Control Officer in the invasion task force that is to land the 77th Division troops on the northern island of Japan at the port of Otaru, Hokkaido.

After the first week the Australian Army had cleared the area in and around the city of Balikpapan and the refinery, then our company moved into the Banoe Hoeke shipyard area. The officers set up quarters in a large square building with four wings extending , south , east and west, this seemed an ideal building for quarters. One morning about 04:00 hours we heard a commotion in the main room of the building. We investigated and found the whole room filled with kneeling Moslems intent on their morning prayers. We had chosen a Moslem Temple for our quarters.

Once we went up river to a large native village and the first thing we noticed in the jungle surrounding the village were chickens. The men made a deal for a large bucket of eggs and a big game rooster. The rooster was so tough we couldn't eat him and the eggs were all rotten.

The harbor at Balikpapan was a beautiful anchorage. A large river flowed into it from the northwest. When the Japanese occupied the area for a naval and shipping base their navy must not have been very alert for there were seven Japanese destroyers sunk while still tied to their berths at the piers. Only the superstructures of the ships showed above the water. The ships looked as if they had just gotten tired of the war and sat down on the bottom and were waiting for the war to be over so they could get up and go home.

There was lots of stuff upriver besides the Japanese troops. When the enemy left the area they abandoned their woman, the harem that the Japanese normally kept with them in combat areas. One day the men captured a Japanese merchant ship upriver and towed it back to the harbor. If they could have gotten up a full head of steam, I am sure they would have brought it in under it's own power. The following week they came in with a Japanese gunboat. Both these boats were heavily camouflaged and had only a small crew on board.

The day before we heard that the Japanese had asked for peace, we had taken an Australian Infantry company up the Koeti river. The next day at 18:00 hours we heard the war was over, but at 22:00 hours we got an urgent message to come immediately and rescue the infantry company.

View from a Company "A" gunboat on the Riko River near Balikpapan, Borneo. This river is loaded with Japanese. Photo courtesy of Loren Aicher.

Infantry of the 1st Australian Corp., 7th Division, 18th Brigade; Company CO at Balikpapan, Borneo, firing at Japanese positions from Belinda tanks. US Army Signal Corp. photo. Photographer: Haas. Photo courtesy the National Archives SC-266424. Photo taken August 29, 1945.

They were being over run by a superior force of the enemy. The gunboats and LCMs headed up river. The Japanese allowed us upriver without a fight. We picked up the Australian troops, but we had to fight our way back down river on the return trip.

The war for the Japanese on Borneo lasted until December. They had been cut off from the outside world and Japan since their radio facilities were destroyed on the first day of the invasion. There was no way for them to verify that the war was really over.

T/4 Henry R. Payne, Company "A," 593rd EB&SR, remembers the assault operations at Balikpapan, Borneo, 1 July 1945, as told to his granddaughter.

SO, GRAND DAUGHTER, THIS IS HOW I WON THE WAR. As I sat, comfortably, with one leg crossed over the other, and feet resting on a soft Ottoman, reading Winston C. Churchill's "Great Battles and Leaders of the Second World War," two small hands came to rest on my knee. Two inquisitive eyes looked up at me and asked, "What are you reading, Grandpa?" "I'm reading about the great men whose deeds and heroic bearing brought about the end of a great World Upheaval."

"They are all in this book," I continued. "Is your name in the book, Grandpa?" she asked. "No, I answered, and I shall speak to them rather harshly about it too." "Well, tell me how you won the war again," she continued. So I promptly laid my book aside and searched the corners of my mind for the years of my lost past youth.

We, that is, Company "A," 593rd EB&SR were a component of the Third Amphibious Brigade, and we had been regrouping and outfitting for the third assault on the Japanese held island of Borneo. Our staging area had been a small island just off the northernmost island of the Molluccan Archipelago, the island of Morotai. This small isle is in the Molluccan Strait, between Morotai and the much larger island of Halmahera. Halmahera still maintained some Japanese resistance at this time and there was confrontation by our troops with these forces. These islands were the fabled "Spice Islands of the Spanish and Portuguese trade," but now they are anything but friendly.

The flotilla that we were to become a part of was composed of shallow draft and agile navy ships. Mostly it consisted of Destroyers, Destroyer Escorts, Mine Sweepers and Two Landing Ship Docks (LSD), which would be our mode of transport to Borneo. These vessels were to sail west through the Kepulauan Sangihe and into the Celebes Sea, hence south to the Makassar Straits, where it assumed the larger ships of the line would be standing offshore, because they had just supported the landing at Samarinda with other elements of our Brigade.

The Landing Ship Dock, number 7, the "Cordell Hull" had its well already filled with water and was awaiting our arrival. The LCMs which we operated would then back into the well deck three abreast and usually ten in line. Once the boats were snug inside, the water would be pumped out leaving the flat bottom landing craft to rest on their propeller protecting skegs. Once this was accomplished, the vessel was set to sail, upon receiving its order. "Destination Balikpapan, Borneo."

This operation, one of a mixed nature, the naval forces would transport Army personnel, who in turn man landing craft in the support of and become the transportation of Australian ground forces into the landing areas. In this nature, the operation was no more off than the others in which we had participated. We had worked with Fuzzy Wuzzies, Marines, Army ground forces as well as Australian forces before. However, the assaults on Borneo had been designed as an Australian Operation by the Allied Supreme Headquarters of General MacArthur, leaving the Philippine Operation to the American forces and assuring the prophecy of General MacArthur that "I shall return" would become a reality.

Our approach to the landing site at Balikpapan was done at night with the ships of the line already shelling the beach sites. The Air Force had been bombing the area for some time previously and their precision could be seen from as far away as fifty miles from the shore. The sky was as bright as a rising sun, with the burning of crude oil stored in the refineries, now ablaze, set afire from both the naval shelling as well as by the Air Force precision bombing. That the fuel storage tanks were afire

Wounded Australian soldiers being taken aboard an American LCM at Balikpapan for a trip to a nearby American hospital ship.

The wounded Australians being transferred to an American hospital ship from an LCM near Balikpapan, Borneo.

Australian wounded being carried from the surf at Balikpapan onto an American LCM for transferral to an American hospital ship.

seemed quite appropriate at the time, since it was almost the 4th of July. After being up half the night, filled with awe and admiration for the precision marksmanship of the big ships guns and recoiling at the concussion of their reports, we were anticipating being launched at first light. However, this did not occur as was expected, it seems that the big guns were to have a field day and display their capabilities before allowing anyone else to assume their role in the landing. This could have been due to suspected gun emplacements ashore and manned by a large compliment of Japanese troops.

The battle plans were to have the large ships parallel the beachhead and deliver their salvos of large caliber guns as the initial offense. They would enter at a predetermined point off to the left of our position and discharge their salvos. They would continue in this manner until reaching another predetermined point off to our right, then turn out to sea. They would then be replaced with another large vessel who would follow in this manner, and the cycle would be repeated. This plan was followed throughout most of the night and into the daylight hours. LCI gunships equipped with 4.5 rocket launchers were next to launch their salvos into the beachhead, but they did so in a parallel line with their bow forward towards the beach. The next parallel line was composed of the destroyers, and amongst these were the Landing Ship Docks, further out were the Troop Transports and the Hospital Ship standing by to handle wounded if and when needed.

After being loaded with troops, the LCMs milled about as if waiting for an undetermined signal to proceed landward. When one started, all seemed just as eager to follow suit. It wasn't very well organized, yet no one lagged very far behind. A second wave followed a few hundred yards behind, and still a third. The sea was rather hostile in its nature, yet it was relatively calm, for the surf was not heavy. What was more surprising was the amount of explosives encountered, relatively close to the beach. The area was well mined and metal barricades were discovered at low tide. The first two LCMs were met with disaster, this was due to hidden mines. However, these crew members were picked up by other boats, although these crews were traumatized by the incident. No reported casualties on the part of the Australian ground troops at this time. Later into the landing period, one LCM did encounter a large mine and met a deadly fate in this incident, both the boat and the crew were lost.

As if things weren't hectic enough, as I headed into the beach, I managed to look up at a low flying P-38 Lightning fighter plane just in time to see the pilot bail out and flow down to join our party. I promptly steered toward him with the intent to pick him up. However, the "Suzy Q," another LCM got to him first and with a wet, but thankful pilot, proceeded to complete its mission. In a later report, he had been delivered to the hospital ship for observation.

Once all troops had been disembarked and delivered beachside, the problem of logistics began. The additional ammunition and provisions, etc., was next on the agenda. In order to receive their orders, the LCMs would come by the Command LCM to read and receive these specific details. These were posted on a large black board on the deck of the Command boat. This vessel had the entire well deck covered by a flat platform shored up by wood cross beams and covered by plywood and canvas. This was done in order to accommodate gunmounts and 4.5 Rocket launchers, while the lower deck served as a snug Radio Communication Center. The Command LCM had been anchored some thousand or so yards from the beach in a "by the stern" type of mooring. It was just some two hundred yards or so off the side of a Navy escort vessel also anchored stern to, and was possibly the overall Command Ship in the immediate landing area.

It was in this setup of vessels that during a lull in the action, that I pulled up to and moored alongside the Command LCM. I could not have been there very long, for I had just started talking to a young Lieutenant, who had recently joined our company (this was Lieutenant James A. Pounds, the co-author of this book). It was during the exchange of greetings that I observed, over his left shoulder, a large splash in the water and turned about and saw a similar splash between our position and the naval vessel. Pointing this out to the Lieutenant, for his observation, and also making note that the naval vessel had moved out dragging anchor, I made it known that we were under fire from the shore and should take immediate action. He quickly complied and ordered the Command LCM to get underway. I yelled out, relaying his orders and promptly headed for my boat. The first shell hit the rear of the Command LCM before I could get away. Looking at where we had just stood, I could

Brigadier General Courtney Whitney, Chief of Civilian Affairs on the staff of General MacArthur, is shown greeting high ranking Australian officers on the deck of a U.S. warship before the party leaves to inspect the invasion beachhead. With Gen. Whitney are, l to r: Gen. Leslie Morshead, CG, Australian 1st Corps.; Maj. Gen. E. J.Milford, CG, Australian 7th Division; and Air Vice Marshall W.D. Bostwick, wearing braid. (Off shore of Balikpapan, Borneo). US Army Signal Corps. photo. Photographer: Fallace. Photograph courtesy of the National Archives SC-339361.

An Islamic mosque next to the shipyard at Balikpapan, Borneo, July or August 1945. Photo courtesy of Henry Payne.

Spotting a land mine on Balikpapan, 1945. (A half-buried artillery shell). Photo courtesy of Edmund Mieszkowski.

see the machine gun and gun mount had landed fully upon the Lieutenant that I had just been talking to. Somehow a piece of debris hit me behind my left ear and into my hairline, since I was bending over to start my engines, I missed being seriously hurt. The damage was not even noticed until later when I discovered my shirt soaked in blood. I still count my blessings for not being in the wrong place that time. Someone hacked the anchor rope and the LCM promptly departed for the Hospital Ship to deliver its casualties. It turned out that all the crew climbed the ladder and stayed with the Hospital Ship. Someone else ran the LCM aground into the beach, where it was promptly repaired by the maintenance crew, and relaunched.

It was some days later, that Sargeant James Ray Lamb, my platoon leader, who gave me the order to take the Command LCM and head into the harbor area of Balikpapan proper. When we, and several other LCMs followed in single file, the Navy Minesweepers was still doing their duty in the main harbor. We turned the point and headed to what was a beach just below a promontory point where it was suspected the Captain of the Port would have his building. The devastation of the area was so complete that the only edifice still standing was a tower in that area. This could have been an enemy artillery or mortar observation point, for as we scrambled ashore to see the only paved macadam road in several years, we were met by an Australian patrol working with sappers and they promptly reported having encountered enemy fire in a tunnel just a couple of hundred yards to our front.

We had not more than exchanged greetings and warnings, when all of us came under mortar fire. Some twenty or so rounds were fired, none doing any damage to personnel or to our LCM. This seemed like the last hurrah for the enemy troops as we were shortly dispatched to a shipyard further into the back part of the bay. It was noted then that only the Dutch Hospital and Convent, plus a Mosque and some lesser houses were not subjected to shell fire. In total, the area became very quiet and peaceful and it was here that the war ended for me. I soon received orders to go home. So, there you have it, young lady, when you become the first woman President of the United States, you can tell your constituents "That it was your grandfather's generation that saved the world from Nazism, Fascism, and Communism."

Richard M. Ledwith, a Cook in Company "A," 593rd EB&SR remembers the war in the assault operation at Balikpapan, Borneo, on 1 July 1945.

There were supposed to be six thousand Japanese Marines to guard the oil at Balikpapan. They retreated up the Samarinda river where the oil wells were located. After the surrender I talked to a Nip officer who could speak real good English, he was a merchant at Singapore for eight years. He told me that their intelligence told them there was going to be three American divisions in the landings so they didn't put up a great fight. He said if they had known there was only going to be one Australian division or army, we never would have landed. As it turned out, I personally experienced the most combat on D-day, I was in the advance detail to help set up our company area. It was a full scale landing, a big convoy. The beach was bombed and shelled until you could not have imagined anything could be left alive. The area was fortified by the Dutch, then the Japanese, so it could be well defended.

Our area was on the left flank of the landing beaches and soon the Japanese zeroed in on us with a mortar attack. There was a couple a hundred yards of flat area from the beach and then the hills started to rise. The Japanese were up in the hills in trenches and caves looking down on the beach landing areas. They could see us but we could not see them. There were plenty of craters around us so we did not get hit, but as it was getting dark we feared a counter attack. All night the Australian division fought with flares from both sides. The Australians had Matilda tanks with gun barrels that looked like cannons but they were really flame throwers that could shoot a flame of jellied gasoline a hundred yards or more and they were very effective.

A couple of days after the landing I was part of the crew of one of the three LCMs that went into the bay. We had just gotten well into the bay when a Japanese five inch, dual purpose artillery piece started shooting at us from almost a mile away. They fired seven or eight rounds point blank but they went over us and by this time the gun was knocked out by a P-38 fighter plane.

Instead of coming home when the war was over we went up the rivers to bring the Japanese out. This was dangerous work as we never knew if they had heard of the official surrender or if they wanted to die and take us with them rather than surrender.

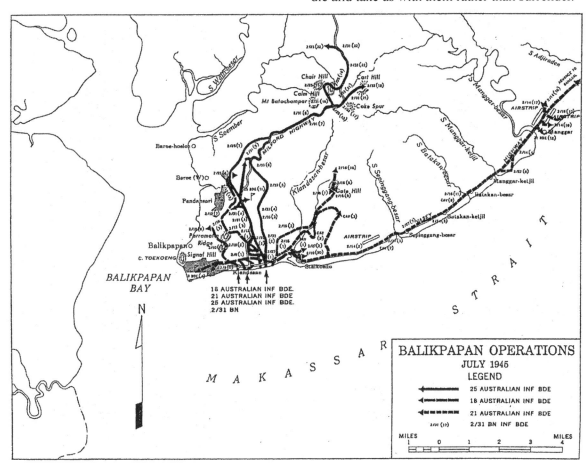

HONORABLE MENTION

The United States Navy Destroyer, USS Charrette, DD-581 was commissioned May 18, 1943 at Boston Navy Yard. Its length was 376 feet, beam 40 feet. It carried five 5 inch guns, five twin 40 mm guns, seven 20 mm guns, two torpedo launchers, each with 5 torpedoes, depth charge racks on the stern and K guns off the sides. Main engines were two sets of GE steam turbines supplied by four Babcock and Wilcox boilers.

She sailed from Subic Bay in the Philippines with Task Force 74.3. On June 5, 1945 the Charrette's mission was to support the invasions of Borneo by Australian troops. On June 7, 1945, she arrived near Brunei Bay, Borneo. Three Australian officers came aboard with their radio gear and set up

in the Charrette's Combat Communication Center to communicate with their troops. The Charrette bombarded the inland area when called for by the spotters for the next three days.

On June 10, 1945, the Charrette participated in the invasion of Brunei Bay. She manned her battle stations all day, providing artillery support with her five inch guns for the Aussie troops on shore. In the afternoon, they called for rapid fire and the Charrette's gun crews responded by firing 500 rounds in three hours. The ship's crew had to cool the barrels with salt water to keep the paint and canvas apron from burning. On June 11, 1945, the Charrette provided artillery support for the next five days. On June 14, 1945, while anchored offshore, a Japanese single engine plane attempted to bomb her, but the enemy plane was shot down by an Allied P-51 fighter plane. On July 1, 1945, the Charrette participated in the invasion of Balikpapan, Borneo. From July 2 until the 8th of July 1945, she provided artillery fire support to the troops on shore. On July 9, 1945, the Charrette, DD-581 departed the Balikpapan area.

During World War II, the Charrette was credited with sinking one Japanese submarine, two destroyers, three cargo ships, shooting down three Japanese aircraft, capturing the Tachibana Maru and taking a total of 1,776 Japanese as prisoners of war. For her combat efforts, she was awarded 13 battle stars.

The Other Units Of The Brigade And The Regiment That Also Served In Combat In Borneo.

We must never forget the other units that supported the boat crews in combat. In addition to the three boat companies of the 1st Battalion of the 593rd Engineer Boat & Shore Regiment that participated in the three Oboe assault operations in Borneo, there were other units of the battalion that served in an essential capacity. The battalion and regimental headquarters companies provided not only administrative control of the operations, they were responsible for medical and communication support. Each operation was assigned a medical detachment to provide for the Wounded and sick. The signal section furnished all communication control.

These were the unsung heroes of the boat battalion operations. The medical personnel established aid stations immediately upon arrival on the beaches. To maintain their services under battle conditions was at times very difficult. Radio and telephone communication was a twenty four hour duty for the signal section. They were responsible for maintaining contact with all elements of the amphibious operation, not only with battalion and regiment but with all Allied troops.

The Amphibious Tractor units and the Engineer Maintenance Detachments were an essential part of the assault landings. The tractors or LVTs were nearly always in the first wave to land on the beach, they were able to crawl over reefs and obstacles placed by the enemy on the beach to trap landing barges. Their duty was to carry in the first troops to secure the beach and provide machine gun fire to cover the initial troop landings. The maintenance detachment were on the beach early in order to repair damaged landing craft, and to assist craft that may have problems getting off the beach after landing. After the initial landing they set up shop to perform complete maintenance and overhaul of landing craft and motor vehicles.

Both the 727th and the 672nd Amphibious Tractor battalions participated in the Borneo operations. The Navy SEA BEES were on all the operations providing their expertise and special equipment in building temporary docks to facilitate the off loading of equipment and supplies to the troops.

The reclaiming of Borneo from the Japanese required the services and skills of all the units as a whole there were no special units. It was the whole team that accomplished the mission and made victory possible.

Company "A" of the U.S. Army 593rd EBSR fighting the Japanese on the Riko River, near Balikpapan, Borneo, July 1945.

94

1. Australian and American cemetery just off Brown Beach, Balikpapan, Borneo, July, 1945.
2. A demolished oil refinery structure, Balikpapan, Borneo.
3. A damaged PBY flying boat on the beach at Balikpapan. These planes brought in emergency supplies and when they landed in high surf, their hull sprang leaks and the planes were run aground.
4. An LCM in the foreground and a burning oil refinery in the background.
5. A bombed building.
6. The Command Post LCM that was sunk by Japanese firepower. It was salvaged and brought to the beach by the boat maintenance section.
7. A view of the shoreline inside Balikpapan Bay at Balikpapan, Borneo.
8. An LCM (landing craft) on the beach being repaired.
9. Beachhead assault landing on D-Day at Balikpapan, Borneo, July 1, 1945.
10. View of the landing beach near the on-shore Command Post, with an LCM stranded in the foreground.
11. The first assault wave of landing craft. headed for the beach at Balikpapan on D-Day, H-Hour, July 1, 1945.
12. A view looking southwest along the beach from Brown beach towards Green Beach. Naval personnel craft beached.
13. The boat maintenance shop set up near Green beach on Balikpapan, Borneo.
14. Looking south along the beach.
15. A view of Balikpapan harbor from the top of the hill where the oil refinery was located. Small craft unloading large ships.

All the photographs on these two pages were made by the professional media on D-Day, July 1, 1945. Photos courtesy of Edmund Mieskowski, formerly of Company A of the 593rd EB&SR.

96

Riko River mission, Balikpapan, Borneo, July 1945. This photograph shows a Japanese gunboat partly sunk by fire from Co. A's LCM gunboat. The Japanese crew escaped into the jungle.

3-latch , 150 foot, 500 ton Japanese freighter captured on Riko River Mission, Balikpapan, Borneo, July 1945. Ship is being towed full of cargo of clothing, coal and petroleum to Balik Bay.

97

A Japanese military cemetery on Balikpapan, Borneo, July 1945. Fire bombs gave this place a going over.

Japanese prisoners along the Riko river, near Balikpapan, Borneo, July 1945.

CHAPTER 8

Japanese Surrender
On Borneo

Japanese pilot surrendering on Labuan Island, Borneo, in
1945. Photo courtesy of Laurette Gosselin. Photo originally
owned by the late Armand Gosselin.

The crew of the Japanese
surrender plane at the Labuan
Island airfield, Brunei Bay,
Borneo, 1945. Photo courtesy of
Hoket Ayscue.

The Japanese General sitting in an American jeep, waiting to sign the surrender terms on Labuan Island, Borneo, in 1945. Photo courtesy of Hoket Ayscue.

A Japanese interpreter talking with an Australian corporal, while the Japanese general stands by at the surrender negotiations held on Borneo. Photo courtesy of Welton Stein.

Japanese Surrender On Borneo

On 2 September 1945, the Japanese Government unconditionally surrendered in a war ending ceremony aboard the American battleship USS Missouri, while anchored in Tokyo Bay. This surrender officially ended the hostilities in the Pacific between the Allies and Japan but many of the Japanese field troops did not surrender until later. Portions of the Japanese 37th Army did not capitulate until they were overcome by Australian Special Forces at the end of October 1945.

General Imamuro and Vice Admiral Kusaka, commanders of the Rabaul, New Britain Forces surrendered to General Sturdes on 6 September. On 8 September, Vice Admiral Kamada surrendered all Japanese forces in Dutch New Guinea to Major General Milford, commanding officer of the 7th Australian Division. Lieutenant Colonel Robson accepted the surrender of Major General Uno at Bandjermasin, Borneo. There was another surrender on 8 September at Bougainville. General Blamey accepted the surrender of the Japanese 2nd Army's Lieutenant General Teshima on Morotai Island on 9 September. On 12 September, Lieutenant General Adachi of the 18th Japanese Army surrendered in New Guinea. General Wooten accepted the surrender of Lieutenant General Baba's 37th Army on Labuan Island. Then there were surrenders at Wewak, Papua New Guinea, at Kuching, Borneo and Singapore. Since the Australian Armies were charged with the duties of clearing by-passed pockets of the enemy, it became their lot to accept the surrender of these areas.

The following is a memo from Regimental Headquarters to 3rd Brigade Headquarters informing them of the surrender Negotiations in the Balikpapan Area.

```
Headquarters
593rd Engineer Boat and Shore
Regiment 3rd Engineer Special
Brigade
APO 928 31 October 1945.

SUBJECT: Surrender Negotiatons.
Balikpapan Area.
TO: Commanding Officer, 3rd
Engineer
```

```
Special Brigade, APO 928.

1.  Enclosed is an account by
Captain John C. Seale, commanding
"A" company, 593rd EB&SR,
extracted from "A" company
operation report and forwarded
for your information, describing
initial contact with enemy
forces in the Balikpapan Area by
Allied Officials for surrender
negotiations.

FOR THE COMMANDING OFFICER:
sg. Zachary Buchalter
```

The following is the "Account of Surrender Negotiations, Balikpapan Area," 10 September 1945.

On 3 September 1945, the gunboat M9G3; crewed by T/4 Phalon, T/5 Comer, T/5 Eckstein, T/4 Boynton and T/5 Weter and the MgA15, crewed by T/4 Dotzler, T/5 DuJardin, PFC Dow and PFC Wolfe, departed from this base to make the first formal peace negotiations, in this area, with the Japanese. Lt. Kluba was mission leader and T/Sgt Titus and S/Sgt Black were the Non Commissioned Officers. Three Australian Officers were present to conduct negotiations, they were Captain Jacobson, Captain Smith, and Lieutenant Smith of the 7th Division Headquarters. "A" company personnel were dressed in suntans and carried arms. The men were not at the gun during the trip upriver, but were in a position where no time would be lost getting the guns into action. The two LCMs proceeded up the Semoi River to Semoi Village where the first Japanese were sighted. Two Japanese enlisted men on shore motioned the gunboat to beach at the river bank, but the Amphibs elected to make fast to a Japanese barge moored against the shore. Japanese asked that negotiations be conducted ashore, but again the Japanese desires were not adhered to and negotiations were held on the deck of the gunboat.

Upon request, Japanese Captain Endo (Navy) came aboard and he was asked by the Australian interpreter if he were the highest ranking officer at the base. He replied that Rear Admiral Nomiyo Sabato was in command and would put in his appearance in about one half hour. With the Admiral was his staff, consisting of Lieutenant Senior Grade Honda (Navy), Lieutenant Fukutoro (Army), and Mr. Nomada, a Japanese civilian. Rear Admiral Nomiyo Sabato stated that he was subordinate in command to Vice Admiral Kamada at Samarinda and that all such decisions were not in his power to make. He did arrange to contact the Vice Admiral by radio and pass on the information concerning future contacts and arrangements for the final surrender.

Australian war correspondents were present and pictures were taken by them and the troops. The only breach from the strict Japanese stiffness and formality was a request by the Admiral that he be given a copy of the pictures taken, for a souvenir of the occasion.

After the usual bow and salute the delegates were seated on the gun deck of the M9G3. They were dressed in shirts and blouses and wore Sam Browne belts. Each officer carried a sword that he was permitted to retain as there had been no surrender in this area up to now. After the ceremonies had been completed they lined up to again have their pictures taken and they retired to their headquarters. The Amphibs and Aussies proceeded back to Balikpapan.

On 10 September, the company gunboat and two LCMs left Balikpapan for Admiral Nomiya Sabato's headquarters in Samarinda to negotiate the surrender of all Japanese troops in Borneo. Lieutenant Howard J. Gallagher, platoon leader in "A" company, signed as the representative of the US Armed Forces in this area.

Four Japanese prisoners pose for a portrait. They are among the lucky ones who gave themselves up. Photo courtesy of Robert Boddy.

More Japanese prisoners. Note the boy on the left holding the American GI mess kit—he can't be more than 15 years old. Photo courtesy of Robert Boddy.

The following are excerpts from a news article in the "Amphibian News" Volume V, Number 9, 8 September 1945.

Admiral Nomiya Sabato Signs Surrender Aboard An "A" Company Gunboat

After twenty one months of overseas service, the greater part of which was spent in pursuit of the enemy, on September 3rd 1945, at 10:00 hours, the officer and enlisted men of Company "A" of the 593rd Engineer Boat & Shore Regiment tasted the nectar-sweetness of victory.

At Semoi Village, on the Semoi River, a tributary of Balikpapan Bay, in Borneo, five Japanese envoys contacted the headquarters of Company "A", of the 593rd EB&SR with the purpose of arranging terms of surrender of all Japanese Army and Navy personnel in that area.

The five Japanese, headed by Admiral Nomiya Sabato were received by Lieutenant Harry Kluba, the enlisted men of Company "A" and three Australian Army Officers.

During this meeting arrangements for a formal surrender was made. On September 8th, the signing of the surrender document will take place aboard the same gunboat on which the negotiations for surrender were made, the Japanese officers, bemedaled, in full field uniforms, carried their anachronistic Samurai swords and katanas.

War correspondents and men of Company "A" will witness the signing and have permission to photograph the event.

(The above news article is the story of the surrender preparations of the Japanese forces in the Balikpapan Borneo from the American point of view.)

Japanese surrender at Balikpapan, Borneo, aboard an Australian ship, September 3, 1945. Photo courtesy of Willis "Bud" Siegfried.

The following is the story of the surrender preparations of the Japanese forces in the Balikpapan Borneo area from the Australian point of view, and is an excerpt from an unidentified News Article.

Contact At Last With Balikpapan Area Japanese.

Balikpapan, Tuesday. Contact with the Japanese has at last been made in the Bakikpapan sector. Since the end of the fighting, leaflets have been dropped calling on the Japanese to send envoys to the Australian lines, but none appeared.

However, on a cruise to the head of Balikpapan Bay yesterday Lieutenant Smith, (2/1st Pioneers), of Kyogle NSW, was beckoned by Japanese at a village thirty miles up the bay and given a note requesting a rendezvous with interpreters, at the same spot today:

Lieutenant Smith, who had with him two privates and some US servicemen, saw the Japanese near Demai village in a clearing among a maze of marshes. This morning Captain Jacobsen, a former Rabaul resident, who is a 7th Division Intelligence Officer, went up the bay with an armed section of pioneers as escort and Captain Smith, of Adelaide, as interpreter. The party traveled in two LCMs, one of which was converted to a heavily armed gunboat, and were escorted by two RAAF Boomeranges.

The way led through narrow lanes of water lined with mangroves and nipa nipa palm. Sunken in the mud were wrecks of barges and motor boats, victims of Allied bombings. Rounding a bend suddenly, the Australians saw two Japanese soldiers on a barge. They welcomed the Australians and eagerly tied up the gunboat. In a few minutes Japanese officers appeared. Chairs, some of them supplied by the Japanese, were drawn up on the deck of the gunboat and the conference began. The senior Japanese Officer was Rear Admiral Sabato. Other officers, and a Japanese civilian made the Japanese party up to about twenty.

All were unarmed, except that the officers had swords, but possibly there were guns behind the foliage. The admiral said he was only the local force commander and that Vice Admiral Kamada, his superior at Samarinda, would have to give the word

before the surrender was effected. He promised to make contact with Kamada and ask for envoys and was given a wireless frequency by which he could keep in touch with Australians for instructions. The Japanese, although cooperative were not over liberal with information. But they gave salutes to most anybody. During the conference, two Austers paraded the sky and the Boomeranges did victory rolls.

Some of the Australians went ashore and inspected the Japanese huts. One sighted a pot of red paint and a brush and quickly wrote "AIF" on the side of a hut. Just as quickly a Japanese sighted a brush and wrote "NIPPON" above "AIF".

The following is the Remembrance of an Amphib that accepted a Japanese surrender at Balikpapan, Borneo at the close of the war in the Pacific. These two enlisted men, Jim Igoe and John "Red" McGillis, were members of Company "A", 593rd EB&SR and they participated in the D-day Assault Landing on the beaches of Balikpapan.

When the Japanese announced their surrender at the end of the Pacific war, McGillis and myself went up to where the Japanese officers had their homes, in an area where the Dutch Oil executives lived part time before the war.

I was dressed as a US Army Captain and McGillis had on an Australian Officers uniform and we accepted the Japanese surrender a day before the Australian and US Forces were to take them prisoners. The Japanese Naval Officer was a Commander, his name I can not remember, but he had graduated from Columbia University in New York. He had lived in Brooklyn for a while and knew a great deal about Brooklyn, as I did. We came down the hill with the Commander and approximately ten other officers and were met by an Australian Brigadier and Captain John Seale, our company commander along with other Australian and American officers and men.

The Jap officer presented a bouquet of flowers to the Australian and saluted. The Australians laid the flowers on the ground and accepted the formal surrender. Our company commander was fit to be tied and as a result of this caper McGillis and I did many days of extra duty. We were scheduled to be court martialed, but for some reason it never happened and a few weeks later we were sent back to the States.

JAPANESE ORNAMENTS AND OTHER INSIGNIA

Reprinted from Everybody's Weekly, The Philadelphia Inquirer, December 6, 1942

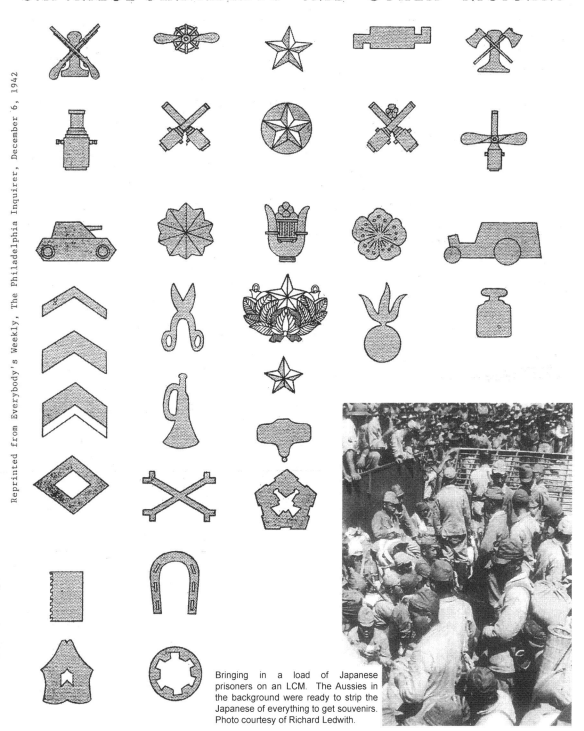

Bringing in a load of Japanese prisoners on an LCM. The Aussies in the background were ready to strip the Japanese of everything to get souvenirs. Photo courtesy of Richard Ledwith.

CHAPTER 9

In Memorium

Here before us are men who were our comrades and friends. They are the men that laughed with us, joked with us, and trained with us. They are the men that were on the same ship with us, men who made invasions with us, men who fought with us and feared with us. We have seen these men killed with our own eyes and anyone of us might have died in their places. Indeed some of us are alive and breathing because these men had the courage and strength to give their lives for ours.

These men have done their job well. They have paid the ghastly price of freedom. If this freedom be once again lost, the unforgivable blame will be ours, not theirs. Thus let us solemnly swear: This shall not be in vain. Out of this, and from the suffering and sorrow borne of this war will come—we promise—the birth of a new freedom for the sons of men everywhere.

Chaplain Lawrence V. Bradley, Jr.

1st Lt Burtch, Gregory
Pvt. Crucitta, Domenico S.
Pvt. Curtis, Wallace S.
T/4 DeGregorio, Morris
Pfc Ellis, Harry W.
T/4 Goldschmidt, Walter
T/4 Goode, J.C.
Pfc Hoover, John W.
T/5 Leduc, George E.
T/Sgt Lilies, Elton H.
Pvt Lowe, Delbert L.
Pfc Manoli, George

Pfc Mog, Norman A.
Pfc Neal, Frank S.
Pfc Oprendik, John E.
Pvt Phillips, Harry D.
T/4 Reichenbacher, Charles
Pvt Reynolds, Edward C.
T/5 Todd, Harold A.
T/5 Venorsky, Frank S.
Ist Lt Whitney, John L.
Pvt Williams, Ira R.
T/5 Wilson, LeVerne C.
Pfc Woda, Gilbert J.

Camp Carrabelle, Florida. Left: Lt. Whitney, right: Lt. Friedman. Lieutenant Whitney was killed in action on Labuan Island in June of 1945. Photo courtesy of James A. Pounds.

Four soldiers from Company "B" standing back of three of the four graves of Company "B" men who died in the last Banzai Charge by the Japanese on June 20-21, 1945. Left to right: Tec 4 Emil T. Tederous, S/Sgt. Jim Fulton, Tec 5 Roy I. Moen and Tec Sgt. Danny Caparella. These four men are standing back of the graves of (left to right): 1st Lt. John Whitney, Tec 4 Walter Goldschmidt and Private Wallace S. Curtis. Tec 5 Frank Venorsky's grave is not shown in this picture, but it exists to the far left, outside of the picture. Photo courtesy of D. Caparella. Photo was taken on Labuan Island, 1945.

Private First Class Frank Venorsky, Lt. Whitney's driver. Frank was also killed on Labuan Island, June 1945. Photo courtesy of James A. Pounds.

Left, William Roger Graham; next to him on right, Wallace Curtis. Wally was killed on Labuan Island on June 21, 1945. Photo courtesy of William B. Smith.

LEST WE FORGET
OUR BRIGADE COMRADES
IN EUROPE

A monument honors engineers who fell during the D-Day landing on Utah Beach in Normandy, France in June 1944. Photo courtesy of the New Jersey News Photos, Newark, New Jersey, with the kind permission of Mr. Donald Davidson (an ex-marine). The photographer: Abraham.

This is the list of Australian soldiers, sailors and airmen who died in the battle of Tarakan Island off Borneo 1945

John Richard Brady	John Edward Carlsen	Henry Wykeham Freame
William Francis Ryan	D'arcy Laurence Casley	Leonard Raymond Gale
Keith Gittus Bradshaw	Raymond Eames Chicken	William Jack Giddings
Colin Edward Cohen	Alfred John Christian	Bill Giles
Norman James Cullen	James Alexander Christie	Francis Munroe Gill
Kenneth Lewis Gordon	Keith Charles Christmass	Eric Charles Gooden
John Kevin Hoare	Alfred James Clegg	Kenneth Grahame Gordon
Thomas James Irvine	Herbert Clarence Clively	Ronald Lindsay Gould
Edmund Henry Lee	William Cocking	Norman Keith Graham
Ford Robinson Quartermaine	Stephen Francis Coffey	Harry Charles Greaves
Clarence John Tully	James Methven Collier	Robert Greer
Jack Stanley Turner	Allan Collins	Collin Lloyd Grono
Douglas William Abbott	John Dudley Collison	Claude Grenfield Halls
Stanley James Akers	Ernest William Collyer	Peter Hale Hamilton
Joseph Edward Andrews	William Henry James Compte	Reginald George Handcock
Ronald George Armstrong	Thomas Nelson Cooke	James Henry Harding
Mervin Walter Arnold	Linus John Cochran	John Anthony Hardy
Austin Frank Austin	Noel Coventry	Eric Paul Harris
Francis Joseph Back	Milton Richard Crawley	John Kenneth Haywood
Alfred Irving Badman	William Ronald Crichton	Archibald Heagney
Forrest Harold Banks	Harold Cullen	Frederick Hill
William George Finlay Barnett	Charles Richard Cummings	Richard Leon Hitchen
Stanley William Bastin	Norman Edward Cunningham	Edward Arthur Hobbs
Norman John Bastrup	Robert Herbert Davison	Henry Harold Homer
Richard Isaac Baty	Colin Kenneth Day	Leonard Wallace Horkings
William John Beech	Travis Wilford Derham	Desmond William Albert Howell
John Stanton Bell	Thomas Currie Derrick	Russell Talbot Hunt
William Betts	James Thompson Dillon	Walter Daniel Hunter
Lindsay Harold Ernest Blight	Thomas Patrick Dillon	William Thomas Hunter
Vivian Charles Blunt	Mervyn John Doyle	Cyril David Hutchinson
Robert Campbell Blurton	Melville Harold Duggan	Stanley George Jefferay
William Booth	Raymond Hardy Dunbar	Alan William Jeffrey
Hugh Leonard Boyle	William Henry Eaton	Edgar Johns
Reginald Stanley Bracken	Arthur Leslie Edwards	Henry Kevin Johnston
Thomas Allen Brannelly	Maxwell George Eggins	Norman Woollard Jones
Francis William Broomfield	Reginald Cecil Eirth	Anthony Stratus Kayes
James William Brown	Jack Abbott Eley	Archibald Robert Kelly
Noel John Bunter	William Charles Evans	Patrick Andrew Kelly
Anthony Leslie Buntman	Amor Herbert Farr	Stanley Albert Ket
Clarence Reginald Burke	Sydney John Ferguson	George Gilbert Killingbeck
James Byrne	George William Firman	Ronald Francis Kitson
David Hugh Caldwell	Trevor Raymond Fitzmaurice	Arthur John Langford
Raymond Claude Calnan	John Goodsell Foreman	Joseph Lantere

Raymond Lawrence
Geoffrey Lawrey
Thomas Victor Lawson
John Patrick Leseberg
James William Leslie
Eric John Lewis
Maxwell Ross Lindsay
William John Lobb
Erick Lockyer
John Robert Love
Charles Herbert Lucas
Lewis Ryland Lunson
John McBratney
John Bernard Mackey
William Eric Mackie
William Henry Maguire
Albert Douglas Mansfield
Robert Graham Maslin
Geoff William Mawhinney
Joseph McBride
Michael John McGillion
Bruce Francis McKenzie
Charles Albert McKenzie
Donald Ward McKinnon
Robert Thomas McLaren
Roderick McLeod
Ernest William McMahon
George Crawford Merchant
Wallace Dudley Merchant
Mervin Minchin
Frank Xavier Moloney
Raymond Alvin Monnox
Keith John Moore
Keith Mort
John Ronald Munro
Patrick Vincent Murphy
Roy Charles Murphy

Sydney Claude Murphy
Colin James Neville
Eric Ward Newnham
John Nightingale
Daniel Francis Nippard
Alfred Nutt
Kevin George O'Neill
Kevin John O'Neill
Frederick Stephen Orniston
John Leo O'Rourke
Thomas Alexander Packer
Hartley Page
David Roy Park
Bennett James Patis
Victor Hilary Patton
Harold Pearson
Henry Phillips
Arthur Joseph Pratt
Colin Gordon Pettejohn
Thomas Denis Priora
Samuel Thomas Quigley
Jack Ransome
Ervin Sifroy Rathjen
Kevin Reddish
Reginald George Redman
Frederick Morrison Rees
Harold John Ridgeway
Ronald Ian Ritchie
Keith William Robertson
Henry Bartlett Rowlands
John William Runge
Victor Arthur Russell
Timothy Joseph Ryan
James Robert Seaman
Cornelius Jerome Shanahan
Alick Sheerin
Eugen Louis Sigut

Colin Douglas Simper
Clement Raymond Simpson
William Slavin
Edmund Sutton Slee
Cecil Gordon Smith
Charles Leslie Smith
Walter Harold Smith
John Sutherland Stevens
Frank Leslie Sullivan
John Charles Supple
George Arthur Teates
Herbert Lionel Teese
Douglas George Therkelsen
Melross Thomas
Victor Charles Thomas
Sidney William Thompson
Harold Tideswell
Ronald John Tippins
Roy Patrick Toohey
Trevor John Tranter
Geoffrey Bannister Travis
Charles Phillip William Trickett
Ronald Bruce Turner
William Frederick Waite Tye
Robert Henry Tyrie
Charles Edward Waghorn
Leslie Alexander Waugh
Clement Keith Weeks
Frank Morris Wells
Kevin Ambrose Wells
Frederick James Williamson
John Wilson
Richard Sextus Daly Winter
Trevor Cyril Walton Winter
Kenneth Woodward

This above list of Australians who died at Tarakan Island off Borneo between May 1-August 15, 1945 has been reprinted from "Tarakan, an Australian tragedy" by Dr. Peter Stanley. Our sincere thanks to Dr. Stanley and the Australian War Memorial at Canberra, Australia.

This is only a small portion of the thousands of Australian diggers and sappers that died trying to destroy the Japanese Imperial Forces that had conquered the Dutch East Indies, but it shows the reader how many sacrifices of Australia's finest men were made in the allied defense against the Imperial plans for domination of the Asian and Australian continents. Let us all never forget the sacrifices that were made by the allies in the Southwest Pacific-be they Australian, American, New Zealanders, Dutch, etc. Their blood was spilled to give us all the freedom and chances for individual happiness that we enjoy today at this moment in the Millennium.

AGNES NEWTON KEITH

Agnes Newton Keith, the author of two books, "Land Below The Wind," and "Three Came Home," was born in Oak Park, Illinois. She graduated from the University of California at Berkeley and later married a British Colonial Officer, Harry Keith. Agnes and Harry lived in British North Borneo, where she wrote "Land Below The Wind." The book was about the people, the British aristocracy and the native people of northern Borneo. She and her husband had one son, George.

When the Japanese conquered Borneo at the outset of World War II, she, her husband and son were taken prisoner and were separated in different prison camps. Her husband and the other British Colonial officials were sent to a prison camp near Kuching, while she and her son and the wives and children of the colonial officials were first sent to the Valhalla camp just outside of Sandakan. Some time afterward, the wives and children were transferred to a camp outside of Kuching in Sarawak. Agnes endured sickness and punishment by the Japanese captors. A rape attempt by a Japanese soldier which was foiled by the other women of the camp almost led to her death. She made the mistake of telling the Japanese commander of the camp, Ichio Suga, of the attempted rape. The Japanese insisted that she identify the soldier at a line-up. She was unable to

identify the culprit since it was dark outside and a storm was approaching as she was trying to remove clothes from the clothesline. The Japanese asked her to sign a statement that she had lied and that her story was a fabrication. She refused and was summarily beaten.

Both Agnes and her son came down with a serious case of malaria while in the camp. Life was hard for all the wives and children for they had to work small farms to produce food for their Japanese captors. They were required to bow and show respect to all Japanese personnel; failure to bow brought on severe beatings from the guards. The women and children were freed on 11 September 1945 by Australian troops. Soon afterwards the men were freed also. Harry joined his wife Agnes and his son George and the three of them boarded a US Navy Destroyer Escort for the trip to the Philippines and from there on to San Francisco, California where they visited Agnes' parents. Agnes wrote her second book, "Three Came Home" in 1948. A few years later the book was made into a motion picture, starring Claudette Colbert as Agnes, Patrick Knowles as Harry, and the Japanese prison camp commander was played by Sessue Hayakawa. The movie was a true depiction of Agnes Keith and her son George's imprisonment on Borneo.

LOOKING BACK

This article written by Frank Snars, who was a Sargeant in the Australian Army and who fought on the Island of Tarakan during World War II, looks back at the facts surrounding the invasion of Tarakan.

In writing the account of my own experiences of the Tarakan campaign I tried to divest my mind of post-war prejudices induced from books. Well researched, carefully compiled and highly critical accounts like Peter Charlton's "The Unnecessary War" and Peter Stanley's "Tarakan, An Australian Tragedy" render this difficult. Nevertheless I find many aspects of the Oboe operations that puzzled me during and immediately after the war that continue to disturb me. Important questions remain unanswered.

To me, the whole Borneo campaign, and especially the Tarakan episode, was a costly exercise in futility. No writer that I have studied has arrived

at any satisfactory explanation of its reason; of its main objective; of the rationale that prompted conferences at the highest level of generals, staff officers and governments to prepare and plan for highly complex and risky amphibious landings and large scale combined operations involving tens of thousands of troops, all at a time when the end of the war was inevitable, if not quite as close as it really proved to be, and in a theater of war that was already obviously subordinate to the Philippines and Iwo Jima in MacArthur's grand strategy.

In a briefing on the deck of the Manoora, the vessel that transported us from Morotai to Tarakan, we were told that the main reason and the main objective for our operation was the taking of the airstrip for the two other Oboe operations. Yet the airstrip was not fully operative until after those landings. In fact that at Balikpapan proceeded very effectively using carrier based aircraft. Subtract from the equation the strategic value of its airstrip and the choice of Tarakan as a key strategic objective, becomes very hard to justify. Given the incredible amount of intelligence accumulated before the Tarakan landing from the breaking of the Japanese "Ultra" code that gave away troop numbers and depositions, to the captured native fishermen by amphibious aircraft crews, many decisions seem deplorably naive.

My mates and I at the time thought the choice of the landing beaches were inexplicably inane. I landed with the first wave and our LCIs had no trouble. I recall the beach as muddy and peppered with bomb craters but relatively easy to negotiate. But as the morning wore on jeeps and trucks were bogged, and troops were scrambling along laden with heavy packs in a veritable quagmire. Moreover, the first landings took place at high tide and abnormally high tides are par for the course in that tidal zone. The large LSTs were left stranded, their jaws agape with no attempts being made to unload precious ammunition and stores because of the mud. It has been described as the most unlikely landing beach in military history. I assumed at the time that muddy beaches characterized the entire Tarakan shoreline. But a couple of weeks after the landing while I was with 2nd/23rd Battalion, I accompanied a platoon that was barged around to the east coast where a small detachment of Japs had reoccupied Amal Beach at the eastern end of John's track. We were there for some days and Len Cox, my off-sider wireless operator, and I took turns to accompany patrols up and down some seven miles of white sandy beach that would not be out of place at the tourist resorts of North Queensland. The planners' greatest concern prior to the landing was that the enemy would send fiery rivers of oil to the Lingkas Beach where we landed just as the Dutch had done to the Japs. There were no oil wells or tanks within miles of Amal Beach. To this day anger grips me when I think what might have been.

The selection of three oil producing districts for the Oboe operations, Tarakan, Brunei and Balikpapan, would point to oil, the one vital essential for modern warfare, as the main reason. But by world standards the three collectively were not large producers and would take several months to return to full production.

True, the Borneo fields were important to the Japanese war economy, and were vital strategic targets. But given the undisputed status of Allied air superiority, these oilfields could have been destroyed without waging such a costly large scale ground war.

Yet I held then, and still hold, a strong conviction that oil and the oilfields were the main reason for the operations. I believe that Dutch oil interests were powerful enough, even at the time that the Netherlands were under Nazi German occupation, to influence the Joint Chiefs of Staff, MacArthur and the Australian Government. The body that lobbied so successfully was the emigrant Netherlands Indies Government in Australia, that contained several important representatives of Dutch oil interest and civil service personnel. The oil message was subdued on the broader carrier wave of Dutch colonial interests, stressing the danger to the stability of Southeast Asia in general, and to Australia, if the growing insurgency on the part of Indonesians, fostered by the Japanese occupation, was allowed to move towards independence. The latter fear was also shared by Douglas MacArthur and other American leaders. The bait, to restore Dutch colonialism for the sake of global stability, was swallowed hook, line and sinker.

The Dutch were by no means friends of the Australians, at least those of us in the field. I deplore sweeping ethnic evaluations like I hate the Dutch, or the Irish or the Chinese as indicative of a small mind. Yet in the few days on Tarakan that I had contact with the assemblage of white-clad Dutch civilian personnel billeted in pre-war administrative buildings, I found great difficulty in establishing any sort of social rapport with anyone, although their English was good. The epithets bandied about by Aussies at the time, aloof, arrogant, supercilious do not, even today, seem unfair. Needless to say since then I have met hundreds of Dutch people that don't conform to that impression. I can only assume that these were a product of the time and of the colonial environment that raised them. I thought their futile attempts to win over war hardened natives to loyalty to Queen Wilhemina and the Dutch flag pathetic. Their very presence so soon after the cessation of action smacked of arrogance and lack of sensitivity towards those that had died. Yet another inexplicable strategic blunder was to attack such a small island as Tarakan from which there was no escape for the defending Japs, that had two disastrous ramifications. It caused the enemy to resist tenaciously for weeks, defending every square inch of territory without regard for their own lives. It also virtually precluded any possibility of Brigadier Whitehead's large Oboe 1 force playing any further part in the war. We spent most of what was left of what was 1945, even after VP day, searching for small sporadic groups hiding in the jungle or trying to reach the mainland on crude rafts. If ever MacArthur had any real intentions of using Tarakan, Brunei and Balikpapan as strategic points for an attack on Java it should have evaporated in the first few days of the Tarakan debacle.

On whose shoulders do we lay the blame? Clearly MacArthur and the US Joint Chiefs of Staff share most of it. It was they who had the plans drawn up and it was they who approved them. It seems that the Australian GOC, Blamey, was not enthusiastic about the whole Oboe operation, and voiced his opposition to the Balikpapan landing. In any case the operations came directly under MacArthur's control. He actually visited the beaches of Brunei and Balikpapan. In all of this the Australian Government adopted a passive and subservient stance. Prime Minister Curtin, always a MacArthur sycophant, was enduring a fatal illness, but his cabinet obviously gave its approval.

Vanity and duplicity are traits that critics have leveled at MacArthur. Many of my colleagues in action on Tarakan believed our presence was nothing more than that of a diversion to occupy Australian interests at home while MacArthur and US Forces occupied the world spotlight in the Philippines and Iwo Jima prior to a spectacular entry to Tokyo uncluttered with foreign bodies that might detract from the glory and razzle-dazzle of ultimate victory. Fifty years on, I am not convinced that they were wrong. We learned from World War I that colossal blunders by military and political leaders may be listed and discussed by critics, but that generals and premiers are beyond impeachment. So will it be with the blunderers of Tarakan.

Yet there remains one terrible case of dereliction of duty and responsibility of which we on Tarakan had no knowledge, but which subsequent research has shown that many military and political leaders in the United States and in Australia knew about and failed to act. They have blood on their hands and must be held accountable. I refer to the Sandakan Death Marches.

SANDAKAN DEATH MARCHES,

SANDAKAN, NORTH BORNEO

Early in 1942, the Japanese Imperial Army occupied all of the major developed areas of Borneo including the area of Sandakan. In February 1942, the British military bases at Singapore fell to the enemy and all the captured British and Australian troops were placed in Changi Prison in Singapore. Shortly afterwards the Japanese commenced to move the Australian and British prisoners to Sandakan, the first group arriving there in July 1942. Upon arrival by ship the prisoners were marched approximately sixteen kilometers to the Sandakan Prisoner of War Camp. By April 1943, some seven hundred British were brought into the camp and by June 1943, five hundred Australians were added.

These prisoners were transferred to the Sandakan POW camp to provide manual labor to build an airfield, roadways, clear jungle and to provide work details where needed by the Japanese. The work was physically demanding, but during the first year the food was adequate and they, were being paid ten cents per day. Soon the conditions in camp changed from tolerable to miserable. With the coming of the new Formosan guards, who would live in camp, a punishment known as the "cage" began. This was a wooden structure with bars all around and, without sufficient head room for prisoners to stand. There was no bedding in the cage, no, food was provided for the first week and the guards beat the prisoners at least two times each day. Punishment for trivial misdemeanors could vary from a few days to a month. During the last half of 1943 and most of 1944 the beatings and punishment of prisoners continued, working hours became longer, rations were reduced and sickness became more prevalent. By the end of September 1944 Allied planes were bombing Sandakan and they destroyed the newly built airstrip. Now that the airfield was destroyed the Japanese had no further use for the prisoners. By January 1945 the Japanese stopped feeding the POWs, their health broke down rapidly and the death rate rose noticeably. By this time the Japanese knew it was just a matter of time before the Allied Forces would arrive in Borneo and would probably be in Sandakan on the first assault on the island.

Late in January 1945, the Japanese chose to move the prisoners from Sandakan, westward some two hundred kilometers through rain forests, rivers and swamps, dense jungle, and over high plateaus to Ranau. Those prisoners first to leave were nearly five hundred Australian and British that were divided into nine groups. Nearly all were physically unfit to travel over such demanding terrain as that experienced on the forced march. Many of the prisoners had no footwear. In addition, the prisoners were laden with Japanese food, ammunition and supplies. On the trail they were only fed occasionally with barely enough food to keep them alive and they were forced to eat what ever they could find along the trail. Many of the marchers fell from sheer exhaustion and were shot or bayoneted to death by the guards who dragged the bodies into the jungle and did not bury them.

Upon arrival at Ranau the prisoners were billeted in crowded unsanitary huts where dysentery and malaria were rampant. By June only six of those leaving Sandakan were alive. Of those prisoners remaining at Sandakan, they faired very poorly. The Japanese did not issue them any medical supplies and rations were almost non-existent. By May, nearly nine hundred prisoners had died in camp. Near the end of April another group of prisoners were to be moved to Ranau. An Allied bombing, and shelling of the Sandakan area in mid May convinced the Japanese to move out all, remaining prisoners and burn the POW camp. Of the nearly eight hundred prisoners about five hundred were moved out on the jungle trail west to Ranau. The sick and emaciated remainder of the prisoners were left to fend for themselves.

The second group to move out on the trail to Ranau were treated worse that the first group. They arrived at Ranau with less than two hundred survivors. Of the nearly three hundred prisoners that were abandoned at the camp after it was burned, seventy or eighty were started on the trail to Ranau but no one knows what became of these men. It was suspected they were only able to travel a short ways before the guards killed them, and left their bodies in the jungle. After the camp was burned and the three groups had departed for Ranau, the last few were taken just outside the camp area and shot. Early on it became evident to the prisoners that had survived at Ranau, that the Japanese intended to kill all of them so no one would remain to bear witness against them after the war ended.

In August 1945, after the Japanese surrender, the last of the Ranau prisoners were taken a short ways out of camp where they were shot and buried. Of all the British and Australian prisoners at Sandakan only six managed to escape and live to tell of the deprivation, brutality and suffering the prisoners were subjected to at the hands of the Japanese. These six were witnesses at the war crimes trials after the war. One Australian prisoner suffered the most inhumane treatment that man can bestow on another human. He was in the first group to reach Ranau and soon after arrival he escaped and was recaptured and when he was brought into camp it was obvious he had been beaten severely. After he was placed in confinement the guards beat and punched him for hours day and night. When it was obvious that he was dying they threw him into a road side ditch. The Japanese made a point to tell the other prisoners if they attempted to escape they would share the same fate.

The Japanese Prisoner of War Camp Commandant, Captain Hosijima Susumi was tried and, convicted of war crimes at Labuan Island in January 1946 and was executed. It was obvious to most of the prisoners that the Japanese fully intended to starve, beat, maim and kill all of them, before they surrendered at the end of the war. This was one of the great tragedies of World War II.

The Sandakan Death Marches and Their Significance to Tarakan. This remembrance of the war in Borneo was written by Frank Snars, a Sargeant in the Australian Army, who participated in the assault landings and the recapture of the island of Tarakan during World War II.

Just prior to the landings of the 26th Brigade of the 9th Australian Division at Lingkas Beach in Tarakan, and throughout the Oboe operations at Brunei and Balikpapan, Australian and British prisoners of war were victims of the most heinous crimes meted out to war prisoners since the institution of the Geneva Convention. Some, indeed, would match anything ever perpetrated in war. All of this took place at Sandakan, only a couple of hundred air miles to the north of Tarakan and Brunei on the mainland of Borneo.

Sandakan, the pre-war capital of British Borneo, would have been a much worthier site for a Borneo invasion than any of the three sites chosen. That it had no oil and hence no advantage to the oil corporations party explains why it was overlooked.

It had no airstrip of any consequence before the war—but the Royal Air Force had surveyed a site for a strip that the Japanese established after they occupied the town. It was closer to the Philippines, Malaya and Singapore, but not to Java. It was as close to the Morotai base as Tarakan, nearer to Brunei but further from Balikpapan. It would have had more incentive to Australian troops as it was part of the British Empire that had not yet been dismantled. (The middle letter of the acronym AIF stands for Imperial). The three selected sites were former Dutch colonies.

My point is this. Had there been no atrocities at Sandakan, or had the Australian Government and the War Advisory Council not known of the atrocities, this would still have been a worthier site than Tarakan. But in the light of substantiated evidence accumulated since, it is certain that the Australian authorities were aware of the marches even if they were not aware of the atrocities. From still more recent accounts, many will aver that they knew of atrocities but not of their terrible extent. As early as July, 1942, a contingent of some 1500 Australian prisoners, designated by the Japanese command as "B" Force, were transported under appalling conditions from Changi prison in Singapore to Sandakan. There they were crowded into huts in a compound intended to house 300 to work in the construction of two airstrip runways and roads. Gradually during 1942 an effective underground intelligence network was developed thanks to cooperating remnant personnel of the British colonial service and especially to 8th Division signalmen and their officer, Lieutenant Weynton, who courageously built from "scrounged" parts first a wireless receiver then later a transmitter. By the end of December 1942 a message had been sent out through guerrilla force contacts on Batu Batu Island giving details of "B" Force prisoners that were duly passed on to Allied Command. From then on regular messages were passed to and from the prisoners through "underground" agents. By mid 1943 some 500 more Australian prisoners, designated "E" Force from Kuching and about 750 British prisoners from Jesselton joined the Australians at Sandakan, severely escalating the food and space problems.

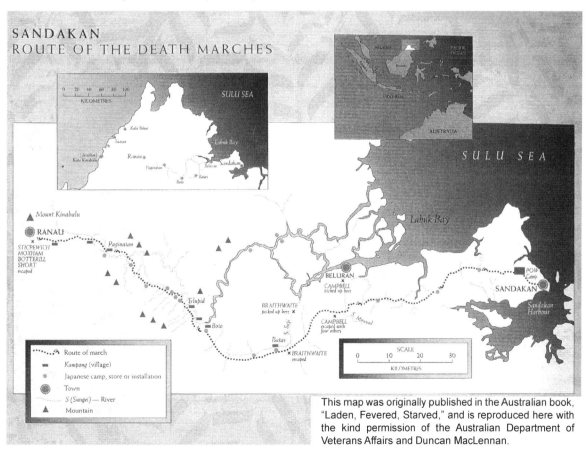

SANDAKAN
ROUTE OF THE DEATH MARCHES

This map was originally published in the Australian book, "Laden, Fevered, Starved," and is reproduced here with the kind permission of the Australian Department of Veterans Affairs and Duncan MacLennan.

115

In July 1943 after the discovery of two radios and other evidence of the covert underground network severe disciplinary measures, and the sentencing to death of Captain Matthews, put an end to the more blatant communication channels with the outside world, but from time to time some contact was possible. From then on the Australian officers were transported by river steamer to Kuching for the rest of the war while the other ranks were herded into Compound One where they were subjected to the most brutal punishment, food rationing, torture—the notorious cage—to an extent that death was often regarded as a merciful release. On September 23, 1944 allied aircraft strafed the prisoners' camp at the airport killing three prisoners, in disregard of a large sign erected by the Japs that read P.O.W. There were no further raids on the camp for six months, when in April 1945 after the Japs had the sign removed, a raid killed some thirty prisoners. Early in 1945 the death marches began. A group of 470 prisoners that included 350 Australians were sent off in batches of 50 each day under guard to the village of Ranau, some 160 miles west of Sandakan over treacherous tracks that led through dense jungle and over steep mountain ranges. Only a minority had any form of footwear, and to a man they were ill, undernourished, and pitifully thin and weak even before they left Sandakan. Throughout the dreadful marches the Japanese guards had copious food and were healthy and fit while the prisoners' food was severely rationed and medical supplies withheld. During March alone 317 prisoners, including 221 Australians died. Those who were left were walking skeletons.

The second death march began on May 29. By this time on the little island of Tarakan only 200 miles to the south, the organized enemy resistance had ceased and the operation was being scaled down. The airstrip was operating. Available now were naval vessels, landing craft, aircraft—Mosquitoes, Mitchells and Morotai based Liberators—and thousands of troops, including commando units raised, trained and equipped for such operations. The Australian GHQ and the Australian Government knew of the prison camps at Sandakan. Whether or not they knew of the atrocious marches that were taking place, they were well aware of atrocities being inflicted on prisoners of war throughout Southeast Asia. Hundreds of deaths were to result from their

indifference to the plight of the Sandakan prisoners and failure to act. Despite their hard campaign on Tarakan, most troops would have relished the task of rescuing their fellow AIF and British prisoners.

On May 29, the Japanese blew up the ammunition dumps, then assembled the prisoners to view the torching of the barracks and buildings. 500 Australian and 100 British prisoners, divided again into units of 50, were marched out. The 300 prisoners, too sick to march, were left without shelter or accommodations of any kind. Unspeakable conditions prevailed for the march. Knee-deep mud and mountain tracks that could only be negotiated on all fours. Those that could not continue each morning were lined up and shot. Many more fell on the way and perished by the wayside. On arrival at Ranau on June 26 only 200—142 Australians and 61 Englishmen—of the 600 marchers survived. They found only six—five Australian and one Englishman remained of the 470 prisoners of the first death march. Most of the first marchers had died since arriving at Ranau, a fate that faced the new arrivals. Most of these were shot by guards or left to perish. A handful escaped, but when the final survivors were rescued by guerrilla forces on September 20 only six men survived of the 2500 who were in the compounds in Sandakan at the end of May. During most of those months two divisions of the Australian Army with thousands of support troops were engaged in campaigns on Borneo that lacked reason or significant goals. Will anyone ever be held accountable? Who cares? Dead men tell no tales.

The Insignia of the "Amphibs" - 3rd Brigade

CHAPTER 10
Borneo Today

The following remarks are from Faye Clarke, who served in the 2/6th Australian General Hospital as a Nurse, on Labuan Island, Borneo during World War II from August through December 1945. She tells here of her return to Labuan Island fo r the 50th year anniversary of the assault landing on the island and these are some of her observations concerning the modern day Labuan.

How different it was to return to Labuan and find a lovely clean city, four lane highways, multi-story buildings and not one rotten monkey in sight. They used to pull our veils off and spit at us as we tried to retrieve them. No mosquitoes, no rubber trees, lovely friendly people who treated us five girls as if we were royalty.

The most moving ceremony was in the cemetery at the sunset, can you imagine the reciting of the "Ode..." At the going down of the sun—and in the morning just as the sun was rising. You will recall the glorious sunsets, even the veteran clergy could barely finish!

Our well-loved Padre, who was married to one of our girls, was shot on Labuan as he carried buckets of tea to the front lines. The anniversary dinner on Labuan was lit with hurricane lanterns and they brought back memories for the only lights we had in our tents, during the war, were hurricane lanterns. There were also memories of our tent collapsing on us during the night in a heavy tropical downpour.

On arrival in Labuan we were quite amazed at the development. This once destroyed island now had a modern airport on the site of the original one. We were taken to our very large elaborate hotel on the other side of the island from the airport. A quick shower and we caught the courtesy bus to the city. It was quite unbelievable how the island had changed and everywhere there were signs "Welcome to Veterans" after fifty years. Six thousand people now live on Labuan. There are still some slum areas but there are happy smiling people and lovely healthy little children.

We were invited to a poolside cocktail party at 7:30 p.m. and here we met up with some three hundred other veterans from Australia and there were many from America. We were welcomed with food, barbecue and drinks and we were treated like royalty. The remainder of our group, from Perth, arrived and the fifty of us completed our group. Such a glorious setting, the pool was besides the beach with palms and tropical flowers, colored umbrellas, colored lights, just a wonderful sight. Bed that night was most welcome as I only "catnapped" on the plane and so at 10:30 p.m. I called it a day.

Saturday June 10th 1995, the actual landing was 1945, fifty years prior, was to be reenacted at Brown Beach, actually was round the side of the island and not too distant from our hospital site. Lots of warships in the harbour, two large oil rigs sit out in the water, these were on the beach when we were there and were burning the entire time of our stay. It was the British who burned them on the arrival of the Japanese in 1942.

The Americans landed amid a smoke screen and the Jets flew over a barrage of guns. We were all seated on a lawn beneath shelter and each was given a small bottle of spring water, as a plaque was unveiled to commemorate the landing by the 9th Australian Division and American gunboats and etc. The local people spoke in glowing terms of their gratitude for the veterans "who turned their lives around." The Japanese had been quite brutal to the civilians and especially the young girls.

A museum displayed Labuan as we saw it during the war, with rubber plantations smashed from bombing. Many of our boys lost their lives but the Japanese casualties were heavier. Morning tea was served to the veterans, a welcome cuppa. At 7:00 am that morning a peace run from the other side of the island, some fourteen K's away, to the site of the landing and these folks arrived at 8:30 am very hot, all dressed in white with a sign on their T-shirts, "Peace Is Best" and a dove holding an olive branch in it's mouth. We returned to the hotel at 11:30 am June 10th.

At 4:00 p.m. we were taken to the Labuan airport where a joint project with the Rotary unveiled a memorial plaque. It was here in 1945 the Air Force and Army built the runway in six days, working around the clock, stopping only when the Japanese bombers came over. Ironically the Head of World Rotary was a Japanese who must have felt uncomfortable to hear of the brutality handed down to the civilians and forces alike by his fellow countrymen. He did not unveil the plaque. From here we went to a sunset service at Labuan War

Cemetery, the largest Commonwealth war cemetery where thirty seven hundred of our lads are buried. A very well cared for place, but a heart breaking place with seventeen hundred tombstones bearing the inscription "Known Only Unto God." It seems the last rotten thing the Japanese could do was destroy their identify discs, but all names are recorded on pillars in the chapel at the entrance likewise in books for easy reference.

I had taken a quantity of poppies from Caloundra, Queensland and handed out some to our girls and we all placed a poppy on our Padre's grave, he had been married to one of our girls and was shot carrying tea to the front.

Memories flooded back as I saw the local cemetery opposite, 'twas there I sat with a friend on a headstone the night we learned the war was over, our hospital site was short distance away. Houses now occupy the land and part is also incorporated into the cemetery. A huge oil refinery was also on the point where we used to swim. A small island just offshore also reminded me of the day a few of us went with some lads and were blasted on returning, as we were told it was riddled with land mines and was totally out of bounds!

June 10th: We returned to our hotel after a very moving ceremony. The sight of that cemetery will remain with me the rest of my life. We were invited to a Gala Dinner in the Grand Ballroom, decorated in miles of red, white and blue material and beautiful chandeliers. It was a wonderful sight with three hundred people present, a very colorful native band formed a guard of honor as we entered

and they entertained us. What a happy crowd are they, but while there was lots of food, fish was out and frankly all their dishes tasted the same and one knew not what they ate, it was vegetables and rice for me.

During the evening a video was shown of a grandson of an American veteran, who returned with five members of his family. It seems the ship he was on as he neared the beach on landing day was sunk by the Japanese, and his grandson, a scuba diver, found the wreck and recovered coins and plates and placed a plaque and a wreath on the wreck, there were beautiful colored fish and a very interesting video. I talked with "grandad"—he could not believe he was back and delighted to have seen his "old ship" sunken though it was.

June 11th: Luggage pickup was at 6:00 am and breakfast was at 6:30 and we met in the hotel foyer at 7:30 for pickup to board the ferry, a sleek vessel for our half hour trip to Sabah. Farewell, Labaun, a much nicer island than the one we knew fifty years ago.

A tropical downpour greeted us as we boarded the ferry and it reminded us tents collapsing on us day and night. Menumbuk, a scruffy post, where we collected by bus enroute to Beaufort for the lunch stop. After a very pretty drive through well ordered paddy fields, market gardens, a few rubber plantations, as none now exist on Labuan, a few plantations of tropical fruits and coconut trees. Lots of quite nice houses, lovely flowers and the roughest roads I have ever been on. We arrived at Beaufort,

A harbor view of Labuan at sunset. Not much has changed in the old town section of Labuan. Photo by the Daily Express, Sabah.

A bird's eye view of the Capital of Sabah, Kota Kinabalu. Photo by the Daily Express, Sabah, Malaysia.

some of our 9th Division boys were camped here and one of our party had been a patient in the rundown building once a C.C.S. Also we saw the spot where the Aussie lad won his Victoria Cross, a monument to him stands for his bravery.

Lunch at a rundown hotel, dare we eat here? But we were told all hotels were safe and although they did eat cats and dogs, none were used in hotels: As the ten of us were seated around the lunch table and dishes of food placed before us, one person, one side said, "Meow and another said Wuff Wuff, guess who didn't eat any meat dishes, veggies and rice did me fine.

It is in this area, that Australian soldiers pushed the Japanese northwards. We also visited the memorial to Albert Wok, a local , who with a band of one hundred twenty three men gave the Australian Army valuable information prior to the landing, they were rounded up and massacred by the Japanese. We arrived at our hotel in the city of Kota-Kinabalu,

we knew it by the name of Jesselton, which was destroyed by bombing raids in 1945.

June 12th: We had a free day, so some of the men folks joined us as we took the courtesy bus to the city. The city was recently rebuilt and was very modern, the water front markets were fun and a very modern shopping center where we had lunch and took a taxi back to our hotel.

June 13th: We left by bus at 8:30 am for a tour of former World War II camp sites. The country, mostly rain forest and with South East Asia's highest mountain, Mount Kinabalu, it was a scenic drive, with forest so dense, we were told by Jack Sue who was a member of the 'Z' Force and worked behind the lines as a coolie, at times he could only crawl on his hands and knees and it was quite impossible to walk. He lay in the jungles for days to count the Japanese convoys which went by train. The Australians thought there were only seven hundred Japanese and virtually no ammunition, but Jack informed them, that trains were loaded with ammo

Labuan Island also has the largest War Memorial on Borneo which commemorates more than 2,000 Allied soldiers who were killed in action on Borneo between 1942 and 1945. Every year "Remembrance Day" is held at the Memorial with a large contingent from Australia. The British come at other times bringing poppies for their departed loved ones, as shown in the picture above. The picture (at the right) shows the "Cross of Sacrifice" which is the centerpiece of the Memorial. Photo by the Daily Express, Sabah, Malaysia.

This is the forecourt of the Labuan War Memorial. Photo by the Daily Express, Sabah, Malaysia.

and some seventeen hundred Japanese troops. Jack was awarded medals for his bravery and undercover work by the Australian Defence and the American Army.

Sabah: Lunch at a very modern hotel and here we saw a video of the "death march" from Sandakan to Kundasung, when seventeen hundred Australians were marched two hundred fifty miles through the jungles, almost starved and brutally treated and many died along the way. At the camp at Kundasung where only a few had survived and was here we saw a monument to a lad who had been tied to a tree for ten days in the heat, no food, no water and each time a Japanese passed him they spat on him, urinated on him and kicked him. After ten days the others were told "he'll die get him", they took him unconscious to a nearby creek and washed and buried him. That night one Japanese guard with a conscience told the rest of them they were to be shot that night and they should run away. There were only six able to leave, the remainder of the men were shot, the survivors were picked up on what is now a public road by an Australian Patrol. The Japanese guards were all hung for their brutality. Our Padre who accompanied us from Beenleigh recited the "Ode" and almost broke

down as he did so, never have I seen men shed tears so openly as we listened to this "death march" story. We went to the monument, erected to these men and there was an Australian garden, and English garden and an Asian garden.

Edie, our friend from Perth, spoke; she had been a civilian P.O.W. at age fourteen until she was eighteen and she owed her life to the Australian Nurses who were also P.O.W.'s. She thanked the nurses and then called us five girls out and told us of her gratitude to nurses and then recited the twenty third Psalm. Again not a dry eye, a very brave lass, who lost her entire family and learned of her brother's death only on returning fifty years later. The next morning we departed for Brunei.

June 14th: We took a bus tour of this clean and lovely place, we first visited the Mosque, so much gold was vulgar, we had to enter barefooted and don a large black robe and we visited the female prayer room then the male prayer room. Then to the Winston Churchill museum that houses the Sultan's chariot. Again masses of gold. On the 25th Anniversary of Brunei, the chariot was pulled by sixty guards with an escort of sixty more all dressed in elaborate uniforms as it was pulled through the city.

Sandakan Memorial Park, Sabah (old North Borneo), Malaysia. A view of the exterior of the Museum at the site. Photo by Duncan MacLennan of the Office of Australian War Graves, Woden, Australia.

The Sandakan Memorial monument at the Sandakan Memorial Park, Sabah, Malaysia. Photo by Duncan MacLennan of the Office of Australian War Graves, Woden, Australia.

An exterior photo of the outside of the Museum at the Sandakan War Memorial Park. The white sign to the right of the picture tells the story of the infamous Sandakan to Ranau death marches that thousands of Australian and British soldiers endured during the latter part of World War II. Photo by Duncan MacLennan of the Office of Australian War Graves, Woden, Australia.

CHAPTER 11
Japanese Occupation Of Borneo

The Japanese plan for capturing Borneo and taking over the vast natural resources of the island was prepared early in 1941 and in November 1941, the plan was activated. The Borneo campaign was to be known as the Kawaguchi Detachment Order. Major General Kiyotake Kawaguchi, the Commander of the Southern Army, who at that time was located in Canton, South China. Additional reinforcement units were added from Japanese troops stationed all over China, Japan and Manchuria. From Canton the Detachment shipped out to the assembly point at Camranh Bay, French Indo-China, arriving there in early December 1941. Their mission, in case of the declaration of war, would be to proceed from Camranh Bay to Borneo and capture the oil facilities at Miri, Seria and the airfield at Kuching, on the west coast of Borneo.

Japanese Intelligence informed the Detachment Commander that enemy troop strength in North Borneo was approximately one thousand regular army troops with about two hundred native troops and probably fifty six hundred troops in Dutch Colonial Borneo. Reports showed the most practical means of travel was to be by water routes since roads were practically non existing. Reliable maps and weather information were not available. Based on the information available, the Detachment Commander realized all troops would have to be trained in amphibious landing techniques. Jungle training would have to be provided and special jungle survival equipment issued to the troops. Only the troops assembled in the initial arrival at Camranh Bay were given jungle warfare training. The additional troops from northern China, Manchuria and Japan did not arrive at the assembly of the Detachment in time for training before the first assault on Borneo.

The Detachment Commander gave orders to land at Miri and Seria on X + 8 Day (15 December 1941) and secure the important natural resources. (Note: X Day was designated as the day that hostilities commenced, or as we knew it as the day that Pearl Harbor was bombed). The first group of troops would land on shore one hour before dawn. All troops would land the first day. All units arrived at the anchorage, an area approximately two miles offshore, at 2400 hours and troops were to be immediately loaded on landing craft for the run into the beach. The Detachment Headquarters arrived on the beach in the second wave and proceeded to a hill south of Miri and erected the operation from that vantage point.

One Infantry Regiment with a platoon of engineers would secure the right flank and land on the coast south of Miri. After landing they were to capture the government buildings, the post office and the surrounding natural resources. Two Infantry Companies and the Special Navy Unit landed on the coast near Lutong and captured the oilfields and the airfield.

A Battalion of Infantry and a platoon of engineers landed on the west coast near Seria and occupied the oilfield area. Some of the troops occupied the sector north of Seria to prepare for the attack on the Brunei Bay area.

The Detachment departed Camranh Bay on 13 December 1941 and arrived at the anchorage two miles offshore from Miri at 22:30 hours on 15 December. On the 15th of December there were high winds and rough seas making the transfer of troops from ships to landing craft very difficult. The turbulent seas delayed the landing operation so that the Right Flank unit landed about 05:00 hours and the Left Flank unit landed at 04:00 hours. Resistance from the enemy was minimal and the airfield and oilfields at Miri and Seria were captured the first day. At Miri, only about fifty police offered resistance and they surrendered with only a little fighting. Most of the enemy had moved to Kuching a week or so before the invasion. Part of the troops were assigned the duty of restoring the oilfields at Miri and Seria. The Japanese suffered approximately forty casualties during 16-23 December 1941.

The landing at Kuching, after the capture of Miri, was accomplished by the use of landing craft traveling along the coast south of Cape Po and west of Cape Sipang. The area along the coast north of Kuching consisted of dense jungle and there were no existing road ways.

The plan for the Detachment was to load into landing craft at dawn at X+16 Day in the area west of Cape Sipang. From this point to proceed upriver southwest of the cape and capture Kuching and secure the airfield that day. Front line units were to land in the first wave. The remaining troops will land X+1 Day in available landing craft and confiscated native craft. The anchorage will be three miles off the estuary west of Cape Sipang. Waves of landing craft will proceed to the beach at 100 meter intervals. Each landing craft will have machine guns and gun crews aboard.

On 22 December 1941 the Japanese Detachment departed Miri, escorted by a destroyer and proceeded westward to a point east of Cape Sipang, arriving at 03:00 hours 24 December. The troop ships and the destroyer were torpedoed by enemy submarines. All ships sustained heavy damage. Troops were placed on landing craft and they arrived on the northeast coast of Kuching at 09:05 hours. Very little resistance was encountered from the enemy. By 16:40 hours on 25 December, the airfield was secured and the enemy had escaped into Dutch Borneo.

On 31 December 1941, orders were given out to attack British North Borneo and advance by way of landing craft and capture Brunei. On 1 January 1942, Labuan Island was captured, then troops marched on Jesselton and Beaufort and took over these two cities. Next city to fall was Sandakan when the troops freed six hundred Japanese civilians that had lived there and worked for the British. By 31 January 1942, Tawau and Lahad Datu had fallen and some fifteen hundred Japanese prisoners were freed. The Japanese had hoped to capture small steamboats and other ships at Brunei but the British had scuttled and destroyed all shipping that would be of use to the Japanese.

Since the Kuching airfield proved to be unsuitable for full military use, the next move was to secure the harbors leading to the Ledo airfields in Northwest Borneo. The capture of the Kuching airfield was considered necessary to provide air support for the upcoming capture of Singapore. Since this field was unsuitable due to its size, its location was in a poorly drained area and the fact that the surrounding terrain would not permit expansion. The capture of the Ledo airfields now became imperative.

On December 1941, the Detachment Commander was ordered to occupy and secure the harbors along the northwest coast of Borneo and capture the Ledo airfields. Troops were ordered to move along the Sarawak river and proceed upriver to establish a route of communication. Enemy strength in the area of the airfields was estimated at about one thousand with machine guns and artillery. By 18 January 1942, the main body of troops were at Bau. Heavy rains at this time created rough seas and swollen rivers making troop movement difficult. On 24 January an enemy force of one thousand men killed and captured

at Sauggau. The Ledo airfields were captured on 27 January. Early in February the Detachment Commander was ordered to make peace in the areas occupied, to set up a military government, develop the natural resources and create a system of self support.

In March 1942, an independent mixed regiment of the Southern Army from Indo China was referred to as the Borneo Garrison and was placed in charge of all Borneo troops. The defense of British Borneo was an Army responsibility and Dutch Borneo's defense was assigned to the Navy. The Borneo Garrison army was originally located in Miri and in April 1944 moved to Jesselton. At this time it became apparent that the enemy with its drives up the New Guinea coast and into northwestern New Guinea could be expected to attack the northern Celebes and that an attack on Borneo could be forthcoming in early 1945. The Borneo Garrison began securing strong points along the northern coast and the completion of airfields was to be completed by January 1945. Orders were received from the Seventh Area Army to fortify such locations as Tawai, Tawi Tawi Island and Sandakan. These areas were to be garrisoned and defended by the 56th Independent Mixed Brigade sent from Japan by the Imperial Headquarters in Tokyo. The 41st Independent Garrison Infantry Battalion was assigned to the Sandakan area. The 40th Independent Garrison Infantry was to be responsible for North Borneo, south of Jesselton.

In September 1944, the decision was made to build eleven airfields located at Tawau, Sandakan, Kudat, Jesselton, Labuan, Miri, Bintulu, Sibu, Sibuyan, Subi Ketjil Island Kuching. All other construction was suspended and all available troops were assigned to airfield construction, thus sacrificing ground defense construction.

Early in September 1944, the commander of the Southern Army added Tarakan Island to the strategic list. At this time the Navy was ordered to set up its blockades on the sea routes around Northern Borneo. In August 1944, a Naval Base was established at Brunei Bay and a mine field was laid at the entrance to the bay. In October the Japanese fleet arrived to await orders to the Philippine area. Also in October, eight thousand replacement troops arrived in Borneo from Japan. Late in October 1944, two Infantry

Battalions were transferred from Jolo Island to

Tarakan Island and became a part of the 2nd Naval Garrison Unit.

The following information is quoted directly from: Pages 37 & 38, "Japanese Monograph No. 26, Borneo Operations 1941-1945, Prepared by: Headquarters United States Army Japan. Distributed by Office of The Chief of Military History, Department of the Army."

Outline of the Japanese Army's estimate of the war situation at the end of December 1944. About 20 October 1944, when the United States forces landed on Leyte in the Philippines, Imperial General Headquarters ordered "Sho Ichi Go" Operation put into action with the intention of fighting a decisive battle on the island. The situation developed unfavorably and in mid-December, Japanese forces were withdrawn from Leyte. The South China Sea was then controlled by the enemy's fleet and the main strategic areas of Borneo were exposed to enemy landings.

It is highly probable that the United States forces will attack Luzon. After completing a mopping up operation in the Philippines, the enemy will then prepare to attack Japan. It is believed that the Australian forces will be charged with the occupation of the Borneo area. It is further estimated that the British and Australian forces will attempt to recover Malaya by launching a concerted attack against both coasts of the peninsula. Judging from their operational preparations, especially the build up of their air and naval forces, the Australian forces would start their attack on Borneo about March 1945.

Our estimate of the Australian plans for the capture of Borneo is: Assisted by elements of the United States Air Force and elements of the British Fleet, the Australian forces will seize certain air bases in strategic areas on the east coast. Simultaneously, they will execute landings at strategic points on the west coast, especially in the vicinity of Brunei. They will then establish a firm footing in western Borneo as part of the overall establishment of a strategic pattern for the invasion of Malaya from the east.

In view of the fact that the main body of the 37th Army is now disposed in northeastern Borneo, it is extremely urgent that the Army promptly strengthen its disposition in the strategic area along the west coast. It is imperative that troops now deployed in the eastern sector be diverted to the western sector as quickly as possible. END OF DIRECT QUOTE

It was difficult for the Army to shuffle the troops to the areas indicated in the directive from Imperial Headquarters to meet the anticipated needs on the north and west coasts of Borneo. The troops from the east coast had to travel over land, through jungles, high mountains and rugged trails. Food shortages, bad weather and sickness caused a great loss of personnel and only a small portion of the troops ever reached the west coast. Those troops that did make it across the island to the west coast were exhausted and ravaged by attacks of malaria and in no condition to meet the physical demands of combat. The enemy continued a unrelenting attack against Japanese shipping of supplies from Singapore to Borneo and the troops were unable to receive any supplies from outside. By March 1945 the air power grew very intense. There were air raids every day cutting off communications from the outside world and denying communication between units on the island. In April, an enemy naval attack wiped out the garrison on Tawi Tawi Island. The 7th Australian Division attacked Tarakan Island and in mid May all contact with the garrison there was lost and it was assumed that all personnel had perished. In June the 9th Australian Division landed at Labuan Island and Brunei Bay and the five hundred troops assigned to the defend the island were wiped out and none survived. At the end of June the Australian 7th Division landed at Balikpapan and the local garrison resisted the invasion for a short while but were soon forced to retreat north of Balikpapan. The war ended while the fighting went on at Balikpapan.

This Book has been passed by U.S. Military Censors for circulation in the United States

JAPAN TODAY

Army
and
Navy

This is the cover of a World War II propaganda publication produced by the Japanese Imperial Military Government in early 1942. English version.

CHAPTER 12
The Coast Guard at War, Pacific Landings

The United States Coast Guard combat photographers at Tarakan Island; Brunei Bay and at Balikpapan, Borneo, May 1st to July 31st, 1945. The following two pages show dramatic photographs taken by Coast Guard Combat photographers at Balikpapan, Borneo, on D-Day, July 1st, 1945.

The U.S. Navy and the U.S. Coast Guard brought into Borneo many of the Australian troops to fight the Japanese on Borneo. These brave men, along with the 3rd Engineer Special Brigade-the 593rd Engineer Boat & Shore Regiment, companies: A, B, and C, assisted the Australian troops in mopping up the Japanese conquerors of Borneo.

This chapter gives recognition to the many ships and men of the U.S. Navy and the U.S. Coast Guard for their heroic assistance in freeing the indigenous peoples of the large island of Borneo-both the British part as well as the Dutch areas.

The following Navy and Coast Guard vessels were involved in the three Borneo operations (OBOE I, VI, and II). This is only a partial list-some names of ships may have been left off inadvertently: USS Achilles, USS Albert W. Grant, USS Alex Diachenko, USS Bailey, USS Bancroft, USS Bell, USS Block Island, USS Boise, USS Burns, USS Caldwell, USS Carter Hall, USS Cloves, USS Cofer, USS Columbia, USS Conner, USS Conway, USS Charrette, USS Cleveland, USS Cony, USS Conynham, USS Dale, USS Denver, USS Donaldson, USS Doyle, USS Drayton, USS Eaton, USS Edwards, USS Fletcher, USS Flusser, USS Formoe, USS Gilbert Islands, USS Hart, USS Jenkins, USS Kephart, USS Killen, USS Kune, USS Kyne, USS Lamons, USS Lloyd, USS Mango, USS McCalla, USS Metcalf, USS Mitchell, USS Montpellier, USS Nashville, USS Newman, USS Nicholas, USS Philip, USS Phoenix, USS Pinto, USS Robinson, USS Rocky Mount, USS Rushmore, USS Salute (sunk off Borneo), USS Saufley, USS Schmitt, USS Shields, USS Scuffle, USS Sentry, USS Smith, USS Stevens, USS Suwannee, USS Taylor, USS Titania, USS Waller, USS Winooski and the USCG cutter, Spencer.

The following Australian naval ships were also in the Borneo operations: HMAS Arunta, HMAS Warramunga, HMAS Westralia, HMAS Hobart, HMAS Lachlan, HMAS Manoora, and the HMAS Shropshire. The following LST's (manned by U.S. Coast Guardsmen) brought Australian troops to Borneo: LST 66, LST 67 and LST 168.

Enroute to Balikpapan. Australian troops wisely stayed out of the sun, using the protection of their shelter halves as the Coast Guard manned LST transporting them heads in convoy for Balikpapan, Borneo. Coast Guard photograph. Courtesy of National Archives. Photo taken in July 1945.

LST 66 at Balikpapan, Borneo. Coast Guard photo #4741. Courtesy of the National Archives, College Park, Maryland. Photo taken July 1945.

Jap Flushing: No covey of quail was flushed more thoroughly than this Jap on Balikpapan, Borneo. An Australian soldier, landed on Borneo from a Coast Guard LST on D-Day is being photographed by Coast Guard Combat Photographer Anker. U.S. Coast Guard photograph. Courtesy of the National Archives. Photo taken July 1945.

Just tykin' it easy matie: Machines of war and men mingle on the top deck of a Coast Guard – manned LST as Australian troops lounge about in a pre-invasion devil-may-care manner. Enroute to the assault on oil-rich Balikpapan, Borneo. The Fighting Aussies appear no more concerned with the imminent invasion than a party headed for a picnic. Coast Guard photograph. Photo courtesy of the National Archives, College Park, Maryland. Photo taken July 1945.

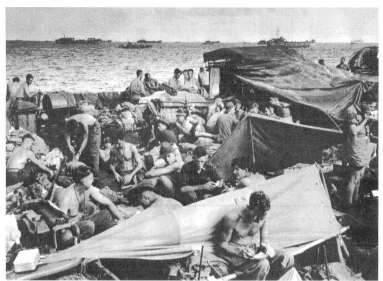

A Coast Guard Combat Photographer, standing in the stern of an LCVP, snaps Australian troops as they storm ashore in the first assault waves to hit Balikpapan on the southeast coast of oil rich Borneo. Heavy black smoke from a burning oil well rolls over the beachhead. Photographer: Gerald C. Anker, U.S. Coast Guard photograph. Courtesy of the National Archives, College Park, Md. Photo taken in July 1945.

Coast Guardsmen land Aussies in Balikpapan Invasion: This is the Balikpapan invasion scene snapped by Coast Guard Combat Photographer James L. Lonergan (standing on boat of picture above) as his own picture was taken by fellow Coast Guard photographer Gerald C. Anker from adjoining LCVP. Coast Guard photograph. Photo courtesy of the National Archives, College Park, Maryland. Photo taken July 1945.

A TROPICAL PARADISE

by Blackie Herrin

Somewhere in the Pacific,
    Where the sun is like a curse,
And each long day is followed,
      By another slightly worse
Where the coral dust is thicker
    Then shifting desert sands,
And a white man dreams and wishes
    For a greener, fairer land.

Somewhere in the Pacific,
      Where a girl is never seen,
Where the sky is always cloudy
    And the grass is always green,
Where the bat's nightly howling
    Robs a man of blessed sleep,
Where there isn't any whiskey,
    And a beer is never cheap.

Somewhere in the Pacific,
      Where the nights were made for love,
And the moon is like a searchlight,
      While the Southern Cross above
Sparkles like a diamond
    In the balmy tropic night.
It's a shameless waste of beauty
    When there's not a girl in sight.

Somewhere in the Pacific,
      Where the mail is always late,
And a Christmas card in April
    is considered up-to-date,
Where we never have a pay day,
    And we never have a cent
But we never miss the money,
    Cause we'd never get it spent.

Somewhere in the Pacific,
      Where the ants and lizards play,
And a hundred fresh mosquitoes
    Replace each one you slay,
So take me back to Frisco
    Let me hear the Mission bell,
For this God-foresaken outpost,
    Is a substitute for Hell!

Compliments of "The
    Anonymous Printer"

To you who answered the call of your country and served in its Armed Forces to bring about the total defeat of the enemy, I extend the heartfelt thanks of a grateful Nation. As one of the Nation's finest, you undertook the most severe task one can be called upon to perform. Because you demonstrated the fortitude, resourcefulness and calm judgment necessary to carry out that task, we now look to you for leadership and example in further exalting our country in peace.

Harry S. Truman

THE WHITE HOUSE

ACKNOWLEDGMENTS

*The following persons and institutions were
most helpful to the authors of this book:*
AICHER, Loren, Somerset, Wisconsin
ALF, Richard W., Chicago, Illinois
ANDERSON, Mrs Betty, Little River, Kansas
ANGELONI, Vincent, Malvern, Ohio
AYSCUE, Hoket V., Oxford, North Carolina,
AZIZ, Azizah., New York, New York
BAKER, Herbert, Whittensville, Massachusetts
BELAND, Paul H., Hackensack, New Jersey
BERGERON, Russell, Westwego, Louisiana
BLACK, Grover, Morehead, Kentucky
BODDY, Robert, Lake Wales, Florida
BORODIN, Paul D., N. Myrtle Beach, South Carolina
BURKE, Dwaine, Stillwater, Minnesota
CAPARELLA, Donato J., Valley Stream, New York
CAPORICCIO, Mario, Philadelphia, Pennsylvania
CICCOMOSCOLO, Daniel and Patrica, Moline, Illinois
CLARKE, Faye, Golden Beach, Caloundra, Queensland, Australia
COWIE, Major Robert F., Ashgrove, Queensland, Australia
CUNNINGHAM, John W., Mount Bethel, Pennsylvania
DAVID, Chester, Cleveland, Ohio
DAVIDSON, Donald, Newark, New Jersey
DAVIS, Mrs Mary, Johnson City, New York
DE BLASIE, Anthony, Hamilton, Massachusetts
DE PRETE, Mrs Mary, Coventry, Rhode Island
ECKSTEIN, John, Baltimore, Maryland
FINCH, Brigadier General Rogers B., Little Silver, New Jersey
FISHER, John M., San Antonio, Texas
FOELLER, Joseph, Green Bay, Wisconsin
FORD, Thomas B., Arana Hills, Brisbane, Queensland, Australia
GOSSELIN, Mrs Laurette, Lawrence, Massachusetts
GRAHAM, W. Roger, Fredericksburg, Virginia
GROSSBERG, David, M.D., Rockville, Maryland
GROSSBERG, Julius, Del Ray Beach, Florida
HABERMEHL, Floyd F., Lennon, Michigan
HARMON, Michael, Spring Lake, Michigan
HERMAN, Albert, Weare, New Hampshire
IGOE, James P., San Jose, California
JUDAH, Sampson D., Forest Grove, Oregon
KILLORAN, Mrs Ruth, Ontonagan, Michigan
KNEEBONE, Mrs R., Perth, Australia
KRUEGER, Victor, Watertown, Massachusetts

LAUFMANN, Wilmer, Howard, South Dakota
LEDWITH, Richard, Sacramento, California
LEGGETT, James J., Elizabeth, New Jersey
LINDSEY, Lewis, Rome, Georgia
LIT, Joseph B., Boynton, Beach, Florida
MACLENNAN, Duncan, Woden, Australia
McAFEE, Joseph J., West Point, New York
McMURCHY, Walter P., Vicksburg, Mississippi
MARCH, John J., St. Lucia, Brisbane, Queensland, Australia
MEAGHER, George E., Charleston, South Carolina
MEAUX, Pervis, Abbeville, Louisiana
MEDVEC, William A., Sand Coulee, Montana
MERRILL, James C., Bakersfield, California
MICHELS, Bernard, Aurora, Illinois
MICHELSON, Nathan, Valley Stream, New York
MIESZKOWSKI, Edmund, Brookfield, Wisconsin
MUSCHINSKE, Leroy, Oak Creek, Wisconsin
NAISH, Mrs Mary, Pomona, California
N.I.C.A. (Netherlands Indies Civilian Authority)
O'BRIEN, J. Philip, Graceville, Brisbane, Queensland, Australia
OFFUTT, Deward L. Millstone, West Virginia
ORR, John G., Glen Arbor, Michigan
PAKIZ, Anton J., Chisholm, Minnesota
PAQUETTE, Ernest W., Grosse Pointe Woods, Michigan
PAYNE, Henry R., Sacramento, California
PEREZ, Epifanio G., Roswell, New Mexico
PFIEFFER, Charles, Maitland, Florida
PHISTER, Mrs Kathleen, Canton, Ohio
PULLEN, Mrs. Mary, Cadillac, Michigan
QUIGG, Bennie, Davenport, Iowa.
RAHIM, Nurul Huda, New York, New York
REDDIN, Donald, Kinnelon, New Jersey
REID, Richard, PhD., Woden, Australia
ROEMLEIN, William, Bergenfield, New Jersey
ROYAL, Toms B., Trenton, New Jersey
SALLEH, Harris bin Mohamed, Kota Kinabalu, Sabah Malaysia
SCOTT, Bruce, Minister of Veterans Affairs, Woden, Australia
SIEGFRIED, Willis E., Denver, Colorado
SIMMONS, Mrs. Mary, Rodeo, California
SMITH, William B., Belton, South Carolina
SNARS, Frank S., Ipswich, Queensland, Australia
SNOWMAN, William H., Upper Arlington, Ohio
STANLEY, Peter, PhD., Canberra, Australia
STAUTHAMMER, John, Pekin, Illinois
STEIN, Welton, Sugarcreek, Ohio

TANAKA, Takeshi, Odawara City, Japan
TAYLOR, Lawrence D., Mission, Texas
THOMPSON, John T., Mount Dora, Florida
TOZZI, Alan, Magnolia, Ohio
TREGEMBO, George, Wilmington, North Carolina
TURNER, Susan, PhD., Queensland Museum, Australia
VERSER, Arthur, San Mateo, California
WAGNER, Shirley I., (nee Case), Des Moines, Iowa
WALDMAN, Marius, Jersey City, New Jersey
WANDER, George G., Postville, Iowa
WILLIAMS, Garfield O., Kingsley, Pennsylvania
WISSE, Thomas, Elmwood Park, New Jersey
ZALOOM,, George, Pacific Palisades, California

AUSTRALIAN DEPARTMENT OF VETERANS AFFAIRS, Woden, Australia
AUSTRALIAN WAR MEMORIAL, Canberra, Australia
MALAYSIA TOURISM PROMOTION BOARD, New York, New York
NEW JERSEY NEWS PHOTOS, Newark, New Jersey
NEW YORK PUBLIC LIBRARY, New York, New York
NEW YORK SUNDAY NEWS, New York
OFFICE OF AUSTRALIAN WAR GRAVES, Woden, Australia
THE DAILY EXPRESS NEWSPAPER, Sabah, Malaysia
U.S. ARMY HISTORICAL CENTER, Carlisle Barracks, Pennsylvania
U.S. NATIONAL ARCHIVES, College Park, Maryland
THE PHILADELPHIA INQUIRER, Philadelphia, PA.
WEST POINT LIBRARY AND MUSEUM, West Point, New York

REFERENCES

ANONYMOUS. 1945. "We'll Say Goodbye," the story of the Long Rangers, the 307th Bombardment Group (HV) of the 13th Army Air Force.

ANONYMOUS. 1977. Dictionary of American Naval Fighting Ships. Vol. II. Reprint with corrections 1969. Reprint 1977. Navy Department, Office of the Chief of Naval Operations. Naval History Division, Washington.

BERGERAUD, Eric. 1996. "Touched With Fire," the land war in the South Pacific. 556 pp. Viking Press, New York.

DAWS, Gavan. 1994. "Prisoners of the Japanese," P.O.Ws of World War II in the Pacific. Quill. William Morrow Publishers, New York. 462 pp.

FOWLE, Barry W. 1992. "Builders and Fighters," U.S. Army Engineers in World War II. 529 pp. Off. Hist. U.S. Army Corps of Engineers, Fort Belvoir, Virginia.

GIBNEY, Frank. 1995. "Senso," the Japanese remember the Pacific War, Letters to the Editor of Asahi Shimbun. 327 pp. M.E. Sharpe Publishers, Armonk, New York.

HEAVEY, William F. 1947. "Down Ramp," the story of the Army Amphibian Engineers. Infantry Journal Press, Washington, D.C.

JAPANESE MONOGRAPH NO. 26, Borneo Operations, 1941-1945. Prepared By: Headquarters United States Army Japan. Distributed by Office of the Chief of Military History, Department of the Army.

MATHESON, David M. 1959. "Engineers of the Southwest Pacific," 1941-1945, Vol. IV, Amphibious Engineer Operations, Office of the Chief Engineer General, Headquarters Army Forces Pacific. U.S. Army Corps of Engineers, U.S. Government Printing Office, Washington, D.C.

OGDEN, D.A.D. 1943: "Put'em Across," the Third Engineer Special Brigade. Private Publication by the U.S. Army. 34 pp.

PAQUETTE, Ernest W. 1993. "Our Business is Beachheads," the 593rd EB&SR. Self published.

POUNDS, James A. 1997. "A Soldier's Tales of World War II." 272 pp. Unpublished.

RAFFAELE, Paul. 1996. "Harris Salleh of Sabah." 305 pp. Condor Publishing Pty., Co., Hong Kong, China.

REID, Dr. Richard. 1999. "Laden, Fevered, Starved." The POW's of Sandakan, North Borneo. 1945, 90 pp.

RIGGE, Simon, 1980. (Time-Life Editors) "Island Fighting," 208 pp. Time-Life Books, Alexandria, Virginia.

STANLEY, Dr. Peter. 1997. "Tarakan, an Australian Tragedy." 274 pp. Allen & Unwin Publishers, Sydney, New South Wales, Australia.

STEINBERG, Rafael. 1978. (Time-Life Editors) "Island Fighting," 208 pp. Time-Life Books, Alexandria, Virginia.

TAAFE, Stephen R. 1998. "MacArthur's Jungle War." 312 pp. University Press of Kansas.

TANAKA, Yuki. 1998. "Hidden Horrors, Japanese War Crimes in World War II." 267 pp. Westview Press, Boulder, Colorado.

VAIL, Richard M. 1945. "Strike, the Story of the Fighting 17th, New Guinea." 244 pp. Jackson and O'Sullivan Pty., Ltd., Australia.

WILSON, John B. 1993. "Armies, Corps, Divisions and Separate Brigades." 738 pp. Center of Military History, U.S. Army, Washington, D.C.

WISE, James C., Jr. and WILDERSON, Paul W., III. 2000. "Stars in Khaki."—movie actors in the Army and the Air Services. 142 pages. Naval Institute Press, Annapolis, Maryland.

INDEX

All place names and maps, etc. in Italics
Names of individuals in Roman Type

Page

Addendum...iv
Aicher, Loren 11
Alf, Richard, W. 11
Anderson, Robert L.................................. 11
Angeloni, Vincent 11, 83
Atchley, Daniel J.................................... 83
Ayscue, Hoket V..................................... 11
B-24 Liberator bombers....................34-36
Baker, Herbert J. 12, 83
Balikpapan 84-98
Bergeron, Russell A. 12
Berryman, Lt. Gen. Frank 53
Bieszka, Richard M................................. 83
Black, Grover S...................................... 12
Blamey, Gen. Sir. Thomas 53
Boat, Salvaged operations..................... 95
Boddy, Robert 5, 12, 82
Borneo, Australians on....................25-33
Borneo, The bombing of 34-36
Bostwick, Air Vice-Marshall W. D. 91
Brim, Lt. Byron A. 6
Brunei Bay 57-83
Burke, Dwaine 12
Byers, Brig. Gen, ... 9
Caparella, Donato 13, 14, 107
Caporiccio, Mario 13
Carroll, P. 25
Case, Gerard R. ....back cover
Case, James Sanford, Jr........................... v
Cavanagh, Captain J..................... 78, 82, 83
Cemetery, Japanese Military 98
Cemetery, Labuan war 104, 107, 120
Chapman, William K. 83
Charge, Banzai................................66-70
Chilcote, John D..................................... 83
Ciccomoscolo, Joseph............................ 13
Clark, Ernest E...................................... 83
Clydesdale, A.J..................................... 25
Coast Guard U.S. 126
Comer, James E..................................... 83
Cooper, Gary 19
Crow, 1st Sgt. James A. 6
Cunningham, John 13, 83
Curtin, John... 53
Curtis, Henry 83
Curtis, Wallace 106, 107
David, Chester...................................13, 52

David, Marge 13
Davis, Joseph 14
DeBlasie, Anthony 14
DePrete, Albert................................. 14, 83
DeWitt, Francis X 83
Downes, W.M. 81
Dutch, The................................... 55, 112
Dyaks, The 71-73
Eichelberger, Gen. Robert L. 6, 9
Escort, Destroyer 60
Farris, Glenn C...................................... 83
Feldlaufer, Theodore S........................... 83
Finch, Rogers B. vi
Foeller, Joseph 14
Ford, Thomas B. 14, 46, 48, 49, 51
Freeman, Joyce B................................... 83
Friedman, Lt. 107
Freighter, Japanese 97
Gabrielson, G. 82
Gordon, (unknown)............................... 14
Goss, J.C. 82
Gosselin, Armand A. 15
Graack, (unknown)............................... 83
Graham, William R. 15, 107
Grossberg, Julius............................. 10, 15
Guldseth, (unknown)............................ 83
Gunboat, Japanese.............................. 97
Habermehl, Floyd 15
Hall, LSD Carter................................. 42
Harmon, Michael 15, 83
Harvey, Philip H.................................... 83
Healy, (unknown).................................. 14
Heliga, Frank, Jr.................................... 83
Herman, Albert..................................... 16
Hickey, William J................................... 83
Hinkson, John H. 83
Hope, Hospital ship 56
Hope, Bob 37
Horinbein, Frederick 83
Igoe, James P. 16, 104
Island, Labuan 57-83
Island, Muara................................ 26, 27
Island, Tarakan 39-56
Jaskella, (unknown)............................... 83
Jenneman, William E. 83
Jordan, Stella Faye 10, 16
Judah, Sampson..................................... 16

Keith, Agnes Newton 111
Kemper, Howard G. 83
Keyes, Colonel 6
Killoran, Harold 17
Kinabulu, Kota 119
Krueger, Victor 17
Kruezeberger, Francis 83
Krygier, Stanley 83
Kyser, Kay 37
Langford, Frances 37
Largen, James N. 83
Laufmann, Wilmer 17
L.C.M. 7, 42, 89
Ledwith, Richard 17, 92, 93
Letter, Franklin D. Roosevelt ix
Letter, Harry S. Truman 130
Lindsey, Lewis 17, 82
Lit, Joseph 17, 63-65
McMurchy, Walter P. 18, 83
Map, Balikpapan 93
Map, Borneo xii
Map, Brunei Bay 75, 81
Map, Muara Island 75
Map, Tarakan Island 50
Map, Death March 115
March, Death 113-116
Marches, Death, on Borneo 113-116
Maxwell, G.E. 25
MacArthur, Gen. Douglas 6, 53, 56, 81
Meaux, Pervis 18
Medvec, William 18
Memorial, Sandakan 121
Merrill, James 18
Michelson, Nathan 18
Mieszkowski, Edmund 18
Milford, Maj. Gen. E.J. 91
Moran, Louis M. 83
Morshead, Lt. Gen. Sir Leslie 53, 91
Mosque, Islamic 91
Motto, Lt. Col. Charles P. 6
Mullin, Daniel F. 83
Murdecki, Stanley 83
Muroff, (unknown) 83
Muschinske, LeRoy 19
Naish, J. Carroll 19
Naish, Herbert S. 19
Narefski, John F. 83
Navy ships 126
Nazar, Paul 83
N.I.C.A. 55
O'Brien, Phillip James 10, 19

Offutt, Deward L. 20
Ogden, Gen. David A.D. 6, 8
Okuyama, Captain 69, 70
Orr, A. 82
Orr, John G. 20, 78, 82
Orr, Ruth 20
Pakiz, Anton, J. 20
Palmieri, Alfred F. 83
Paquette, Ernest W. 20, 82
Parker, W. 82
Payne, Henry R. 20, 88, 90, 92
Perez, Epifanio G. 21
Phelps, Thomas F. 83
Phister, Charles 21
Pickup, Dick 10
Poem, A Tropical Paradise 129
Poem, Those Little Yankee Barges 80
Poem, War Graves-Tarakan 55
Pounds, Isham F., Jr. v
Pounds, James A. .... 6, 84, back cover
Prisoners, Japanese 98, 102, 105
Pullen, James 21
Quigg, Bennie 21, 52
Radzewicz, George J. 83
Reddin, Donald 21, 83
Richter, Richard R. 83
River, Padis 60
River, Riko 87, 94
Roemlein, William 10, 22, 36, 137
Romano, Tony 37
Rose, Tokyo 38
Rose, William F. 83
Royal, Adm. Forrest Beton 58
Sabah, Labuan Island today 118
Sabah, Kota Kinabalu today 119
Sabu (Sabu Dastigar) 34, 51
Salleh, Harris bin Mohamed 10, 23
Schrader, William 83
Sebek, (unknown) 83
Sheehan, James 83
Siegfried, Willis 22
Simmons, Frank 6, 22
Simpson, Lt. 82
Slee, E.S. 25
Smeland, Melvin 83
Smith, William B. 22
Snars, Frank S. 22, 42-44
Snoots, William F. 83
Snowman, William 4
Sparrow, Richard 83
Stauthammer, John 22

Stein, Welton 23
Stelmachowski, John 83
Stevenson, R.A.E. 25
Sullivan, Chester 17
Surrender, Japanese 99-105
Sutherland, Lt. Gen. Richard K. 6
Sydney Leave Pass 137
Szarnicki, Tony 78, 82
Tanks, Australian 33, 87
Tarakan 39-56
Taylor, Roscoe C. 83
Thomas, (unknown) 83
Thomas, Patty 37
Thompson, John T. 23
Thompson, W. 82
Throckmorton, Jesse M. 83
Today, Borneo 117-121
Tower, Clock 74
Town, Victoria 74
Tozzi, Anthony 23
Tregembo, George R. 23

Triola, (unknown) 14
U.S. Coast Guard 126-128
U.S. Navy 126
U.S. ships 126
Venorsky, Frank 106, 107
Verser, Adelia 24
Verser, Arthur 24
Wagner, Jerry 24
Waldman, Marius 24
Wander, George 24
Warrior, Dyak 71-73
Whitehead, Brig. David 53
Whitney, Brig. Gen. Courtney 91
Whitney, Lt. John 106, 107
Wilkinson, Master Sgt. James W. 6
Williams, Garfield O. 24
Williams, Roy 54
Wobeck, William 19
Wood, Capt. Robert L. Jr. 82
Zaloom, Lt. Ernest 82

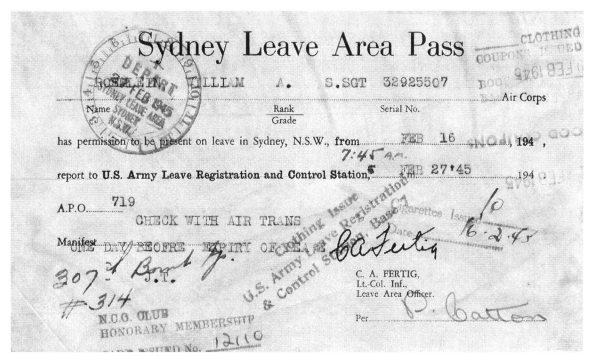

Sydney Leave Pass (courtesy of Bill Roemlein).

Made in the USA
Coppell, TX
05 December 2022

87893474R00090